Financial Freedom at Any Age

A Proven Plan to Save Money & Achieve Debt Free Living... Even If You're Drowning in Debt Right Now - Plus No Spend Challenge Tips & Passive Income Investing Strategies

By

Steve E. Carruso

Steve E. Carruso

investment guide nor investment advice. I am not recommending you buy any of the stocks listed here. Any form of investment or trading is liable to lose you money.

This ebook contains "forward-looking"statements as that term is defined in Section 27A of the Securities Act and Section 21E of the Securities Exchange Act of 1934, as amended by the Private Securities Litigation Reform Act of 1995. All statements, other than historical facts are forward-looking statements.

Forward-looking statements concern future circumstances and results and other statements that are not historical facts and are sometimes identified by the words "may," "will," "should," "potential," "intend," "expect," "endeavor," "seek," "anticipate," "estimate," "overestimate," "underestimate," "believe," "could," "project," "predict," "continue," "target" or other similar words or expressions. Forward-looking statements are based upon current plans, estimates and expectations that are subject to risks, uncertainties and assumptions. Should one or more of these risks or uncertainties materialize, or should underlying assumptions prove incorrect, actual results may vary materially from those indicated or anticipated by such forward-looking statements. The inclusion of such statements should not be regarded as a representation that such plans, estimates or expectations will be achieved.

Table of Contents

Introduction

Debt is scary, and thoughts of overcoming it often feel overwhelming. However, according to the Pew Charitable Trust, about 80% of American households are in debt. But it is not just the households! Businesses and even countries have been caught up in a cycle of borrowing and spending that keeps increasing their loads[1]. Instead of concentrating on clearing the current debts, many simply jump to another line of credit to borrow more.

Many people getting into debt appear not to understand the effect it will have on their lives. However, it is not your fault. That is right. The reality of debt is that life in America is tough and living without borrowing can be really tough. Many people cannot afford to pay for higher education, a mortgage, or even vacations directly from their pockets. So, they resort to loans that also appear relatively easy to get but sink them further into debt.

When you finally realize the debt burden on your shoulder, the following key questions start running through your mind:

- "How did I get here?"

---

[1] Megan, E, 2017, *15 Scary Facts about Debt that Should Alarm you*. <available at> https://www.cheatsheet.com/money-career/facts-about-debt-may-alarm-you-today.html/

- "Am I really normal with this heavy debt burden?"
- "Is it okay to be in debt?"
- "Is my life completely damaged?"
- "Is there a way out?"

Even before digging deeper into how people slip into the problem of debt, it is prudent to know that the journey to financial freedom is possible. Though you are in debt, it can be cleared, and you will be okay!

You only need to understand how to navigate through debt and use this two-part book to overcome it. This guide provides actionable strategies and insights that you can apply in life to make clearing debt easy, gradual, and fun. Indeed, the process does not end there. This book helps you continue with the journey to financial freedom. Many people have overcome debts and marched to financial freedom. So can you.

The Debt Problem: Why you are stuck

While getting into debt appears so simple, trying to get out looks impossible for many people. You might have tried to skip meals or even sold a car to clear off the debt. But, the problem recurred in a bigger magnitude after a couple of years. While some keep saying that it is impossible to live without debt, this book will demonstrate that it is possible to overcome debt and enjoy a debt-free lifestyle.

When you are told that living with debt is normal, it is not true because there are people who have succeeded in addressing their debts and attained financial freedom. This is why this book was created. Here are some things that often make debts look too complex to address:

- **Many Conventional Pieces of Advice are Useless:** If you look at the common methods recommended for addressing debts out there, they are ineffective. Some financial experts out there will write solutions that are simply aimed at helping them drive traffic to their sites as opposed to getting you out of the gutter.

Instead of using any method suggested out there, the right thing is sticking with tested and proven strategies. For example, a strategy that simply requires you to just start making payments will only work in the short-term. Instead, it is important to use workable solutions outlined in this book. The strategies outlined here have been used with great results by people who initially thought that getting out of debt was impossible. This book focuses on empowering you to note the debt problem, understand it, clear it, and finally achieve financial freedom.

- **The figures make the debts look too large.** After taking several loans, such as a student loan and a mortgage, a total debt that runs into thousands of dollars might look humongous. In such a scenario, you are left wondering: "Where do I start addressing the problem?" Unfortunately, this is the wrong approach to take if you want to clear debts.

The proper way to do it is by creating the right mindset. Once you develop the commitment and desire to clear the debt, it will become easy to seek professional help and motivation. However small or big the debt might be, you can clear it with the right motivation.

- **The period required to clear debts appears too long.** When you are applying for a loan, it is common to get fixated on the thing you want to achieve. For example, couples are overjoyed when their mortgage is approved. However, it later dawns on them that they will need to continuously repay the loan for more than 15 years.

Thoughts of hundreds of months trying to clear a debt can appear scary. That said, this should not worry you. The good thing with long-term loans is that only a small amount of your income goes into clearing it. Therefore, it should not scare you. Instead, the long period should motivate you to stick to the repayment schedule.

If you find it hard to stick to the payments, this book will demonstrate how you can stay on top of your debts and personal financial operations through automation. This involves using applications that help with budgeting and even sending reminders so that you can make all payments on time.

- **Poor Planning:** If you do not have the right debt repayment plan, it will be very difficult to get out of debt. Poor planning will make it easy for you to slide back into debts even before getting out. This book helps you to look at your debt broadly and craft a winning recovery strategy.

For example, you should ensure you have an emergency fund and use this book to craft a reliable plan. You are also encouraged to cut unnecessary costs and direct the funds towards clearing your debt.

What this Book is about

When you look at the statistics about people with debts, it is scary. Indeed, a closer look at the route to your current stressful debt status could make clearing it to look difficult. However, you will be surprised to realize that it can be rather simple and fast.

No matter how much debt you have, even if it is more than $100,000, you can topple it. You are not hopeless and you are not bad. You are a normal human being. You can

Steve E. Carruso

overcome the debt.

This book provides you with actionable steps that you can use to craft the right financial behavior, cut unnecessary spending, and become that dream financial icon you always dreamt of. This book pools tested and proven strategies that you will find easy to apply, associate with, and embark on the journey to a debt free life.

The book is broken into two key parts that seek to get you out of debt and further blast you to financial freedom.

Part One: Paying Off Your Debt

This is a comprehensive evaluation of the current debt problem and how it can be eliminated.

- This part is carefully constructed to help you understand the current debt problem and why it is possible to overcome it. It explains that being in debt has become a common thing because everybody-parents, sisters, brothers, and even institutions-appears to be in debt. It demonstrates that you cannot simply wallow in debt wondering why it grew into thousands of dollars in the first place.
- To address the debt, you will have to develop the right mindset and craft a winning formula. However, you do not need to change your lifestyle. You will only

need to make some adjustments and adopt initiatives such as No Spend days or weeks to raise funds to clear the debt.

- Clearing debt is not a punishment. Though you have been in debt, credit cards have a lot of penalties, and your credit score is very poor, these are not reasons to make debt clearance harsh. This part is created on the premise that you can plan to clear debt and still have a smile on your face. How is this possible?

The book suggests fun strategies to help cut down your spending and repay your debt. Think of a 'no spend' day to raise the funds for clearing the smallest loan using your strategy. You simply look for alternatives that are fun, delicious, and highly reliable. When you complete the 'no spend' challenge, shed off an impulse spending behavior, and create a new line of revenue to reward yourself. It is part of the success journey.

- The core of this part is the development of a winning strategy to clear the debt your way. The 4-step debt eliminator helps simplify the process of clearing debt so that you can easily apply and start the journey to financial freedom. As the debt elimination strategy takes shape, this part will motivate you with reports of people who overcame debts and became financially free.

Your case is not unique. Others have cleared debts. You can also get out of debt.

Part Two: Building Wealth

This part was created to serve as a guide to help you start building wealth when you overcome the problem of debt. Unfortunately, many factors that had forced you to get into debts will still be there when you clear the debt or install systems of clearing it. This part serves four key things.

1. It helps you to become a better financial manager. This will go a long way in helping you stay on top of your finances. It recommends that you adopt financial automation and further assists you to create an emergency fund so that nothing will easily get you back to debt.

2. No matter the amount of income that you make every year, this book demonstrates that you can create additional revenue to help clear debt faster. Using the suggestions on this book, you will learn how to increase the streams of revenue and become the successful person you always wanted.

3. To ensure you stay on top of your financial operations, this part also demonstrates how to use your credit card to strengthen your credit score. This will be crucial to ensuring you do not miss important services

by financial companies, telecom organizations, and government agencies because of a poor credit score.

4. As you start investing, this book takes a few steps ahead to help you understand the pitfalls that lay on the way. It helps you to understand pyramid schemes and how to avoid them. It also identifies specific areas of investment such as Mutual funds and Exchange Traded Funds (ETFs) that have helped people reach financial freedom faster than they expected.

Note that getting to financial freedom does not mean giving up all the fun things you cherish in your life. You do not need to forego meals out, make your own soap, or decline social invitations that just came your way. All that is needed is the right mindset and commitment. This is what this book is all about.

The two parts work together to help shape you into a new person. The strategies therein, the demonstrations, and highlighted investment opportunities, will help you to see life differently. The money you have is not little. Rather, it can help to grow your portfolio and make you a happier person.

By the time you are through reading this book, you will not be the same again. You will wish you had it about 10 years ago because it has all the ingredients for success.

Disclaimer: This book was written with the US citizen in the

Steve E. Carruso

mind. Therefore, some companies, services, and apps might not be available in your jurisdiction.

Part 1: Paying off Debts

Chapter One: What Causes Debt

When you take a closer look at the current debt situation in the society, the main question that comes into the mind is: "What made it become this extensive?" The debt issue is a complex thing that has intensified so much in society to the point that people have started seeing it as a normal part of life.

From television advertisements to student forums, the main thing that appears in common to all is debt. People are getting into debts when they are still young but finding a way out appears a major problem. This first chapter explores the main reasons that make people get into debt and get stuck there.

How do People End up with Debt?

The route to debts often commences at a tender age as young people grow up seeing their parents and seniors struggle to pay loans and mortgages. The notion of debt starts becoming a normal thing. But this is not all!

Endless advertising on television channels and social media

shouting *"low credit score is no problem, you can still get credit"* further strengthen the idea that every person has a debt. It creates an impression that you should also not worry about getting into debt because you are part of society. Debt is considered normal and acceptable.

The slippery path to debt becomes distinct when people decide to advance careers by attending college. Taking out a loan is likely to position your balance sheet in the wrong place because you are simply increasing debt at a point when no income is in sight to start repayment. By the time you clear college, you are expected to start repaying the loan. The chances are that your credit score will go down and reduce your chances of getting credit from financial institutions.

After getting employed, you will probably take a mortgage. Within a short while, the deductions to repay loans become overwhelming. Often, many people go for debt consolidation to help reduce high-interest debts. However, the cycle of debt begins again after the repayment burden eases. This results in further damage to your credit score and an inability to access financing.

In addition to the above cycle, there are also specific reasons that could easily get you into debt. Here are some of them:

- **Reduced income:** If your income goes down, the chances are that the expenses are likely to drive you into debt. This can happen if you lose a job or a disaster such as fire razes your business or workplace. When income shrinks, it is prudent to make an urgent effort to align your lifestyle with it. For example, if you used to go for expensive getaways every weekend, consider reducing them or do away with them until the income status improves.

- **Divorce:** Over 50% of the marriages in the United States end up in divorce. Such separation comes with a lot of financial constraints. Because the US law governs how money should be shared in the event of a divorce, the separating parties end up in debt as they seek the help of expensive attorneys to get a bigger chunk of family wealth.

- **Poor money management:** In many cases, poor budgeting results in debt. Many people who operate without a monthly budget find it difficult to track their expenses and easily engage in impulse spending.

- **Underemployment:** When people are underemployed, there is a tendency to feel the situation as a temporary one. Some people end up overspending hoping that a better paying job will help to fill the gap. However, overspending is likely to plunge you into debt if the underemployment situation persists.

- **Gambling:** This is one of the most entertaining

pastimes for Americans today. However, it soon degenerates into a serious addiction that makes you simply want to place the next bet. Many people find the idea of winning millions irresistible even when they have been trying for years without winning anything.

The problem of betting is made worse by the easy availability of loans. Most betting companies do not mind whether you have poor credit score when providing loans. They encourage you to continue borrowing and keep following the big jackpots. Gambling is an effortless way of mortgaging your future.

- **Medical bills:** When people fall ill, it is very easy to slide into debt trying to clear associated bills. The problem is aggravated by the fact that many medical facilities have become impatient and are turning patients into credit reporting agencies, resulting in damage to their credit scores.
- **Little or no savings:** Because of the ever-rising cost of living, the bulk of people's income is being used for expenses such as food, mortgage, transport, and school fees for the kids. However, failing to make ample savings means that you are not prepared for the unexpected. Therefore, when an emergency strikes, the chances are that you will end up falling deeper

into debt.

- **Ignorance:** A large proportion of people in debt
  today are in the situation because they lack info about
  annual percentage rate (APR) on their credit cards.
  They do not know the amount they are charged as
  interest on their credit cards or the implications that
  arise from minimum payments. For example, the
  expectation is that if a loan of $100 and is charged an
  APR of 10%, the cost would be $10 per year. But it is
  more than that when it comes to credit cards,
  mortgages, and car loans[2].

APR on your credit card is compounded to include fees and
interest charges so that the amount you are required to pay
per year is higher than you would anticipate. Though the
loan with the lowest APR is no doubt a cheaper option, it is
important to carefully decipher the calculations and, where
possible, avoid lagging behind the repayment schedule.

- **Lack of Motivation and Guidance:** When people
  recite the route that took them to debts, one thing that
  comes out clearly is that the problem started early in
  life. Many young people, especially those outside of

---

[2]The Balance, 2019, *How to Calculate Annual Percentage Rate (APR).*
<available at >https://www.thebalance.com/annual-percentage-rate-apr-315533

financial careers, are rarely given comprehensive
training on financial freedom. For example, many
financial concepts appear new especially to graduates
in non-business areas of specialization.

Society has to take its own share of the blame. Both Federal
and individual states should reconsider ingraining financial
related training starting from an early point in people
development. At a personal level, parents, communities,
religious leaders, and other entities need to start talking
about the debt and how to avoid it.

- **Increase in Rental Income:** The cost of living has
  been growing steadily over the years but the income of
  most people has stagnated. For example, the cost of
  rental prices in most cities has increased in the last
  two decades forcing people to seek loans to make ends
  meet. For those who want to own homes, the cost of
  mortgages has also gone up. This implies that you are
  likely to take longer repaying your home mortgage
  which can affect your ability to meet the cost of other
  personal needs.
- **Not making debt a priority:** If you are in debt,
  failing to prioritize it in your financial planning can
  prolong your debt and make it worse. In some cases,
  people do not realize they are even in debt! However,
  when you appreciate the problem, dig for more info to

learn about it, and make it a priority, it becomes possible to overcome it.

Important Facts about Debt that Need to Know

To comprehensively explore the topic of debt and how to overcome it, you need to appreciate the magnitude of the problem. It appears that from individuals to companies, the problem of debts keeps getting worse year after year. Here are some important facts that you need to know about debt.

1. **The United States citizens' debt is in excess of $12.58 trillion.** If you toal the debts that American citizens owe on their credit cards, student loans, mortgages, and car loans among other credits, the answer is more than $12.58 trillion[3]. This is indeed more than the Chinese GDP! Of this debt, about two-thirds is a mortgage.

2. **The Standard American Household has a debt of $16,091 on credit cards alone.** If you look at the national debt, the figures are frightening. However, the numbers do not give the entire truth of the actual problem. The average household in the

---

[3] The Balance, 2019, *How to Calculate Annual Percentage Rate (APR)*. <available at >https://www.thebalance.com/annual-percentage-rate-apr-315533

United States has a debt burden of about $16,091 according to Nerdwallet[4].

3. **Car loan delinquencies have risen to 21%.** If you thought that credit card loans are the only serious problem, think again. Auto loans are also a serious debt problem for most Americans. According to the St. Louis Federal Reserve Bank, United States residents have about $1 trillion in auto loans. Between 2012 and 2017, delinquencies on auto loans grew to 21%[5].

However, it is important to appreciate that defaulting an auto loan can be a major problem because your car can be repossessed. This could, in turn, make it difficult to go to work or run your enterprises.

4. **Student loans are in excess of $1 trillion.** When learners take student loans for higher education, the anticipation is that they will get employment and clear the debt a few years after clearing college. However, the plan rarely takes shape. Instead, many students find themselves wallowing in major debts years after graduating from college. According to the New York Federal Reserve Bank, the student loan debt in the US

---

[4] ibid

[5] ibid

stands at $1.31 trillion and takes up 10% of the total American debt[6].

It is important to appreciate that defaulting on student loan could easily damage your credit score and put your social security income into jeopardy. Indeed, even those who are paying their student loans opt to shelf buying new homes and starting families.

5. **Generation X and Baby Boomers have the highest level of debt.** Though millennials could have the baggage of student loans, you will be surprised to realize that they are not the cohort with the largest debts in the United States. Instead, the Baby boomers and Generation X have the biggest chunk of American Debt. People in the above two groups have more than $42,000 in non-mortgage debts[7].

6. **Debt has a positive correlation with depression.** It is not uncommon for people to feel overwhelmed by piles of unpaid bills and loans that

---

[6] Megan, E, 2017, *15 Scary Facts about Debt that Should Alarm you.* <available at> https://www.cheatsheet.com/money-career/facts-about-debt-may-alarm-you-today.html/

[7] Megan, E, 2017, *15 Scary Facts about Debt that Should Alarm you.* <available at> https://www.cheatsheet.com/money-career/facts-about-debt-may-alarm-you-today.html/

require processing every month. Now, this has been linked to negative impacts on mental health. In one of the studies done by the University of Wisconsin, short-term debts such as credit card loans are linked to the high prevalence of depression symptoms. However, the study established that long-term debts do not cause anxiety because many people see them as part of their investment[8].

7. **A lot of people underestimate their debts.** While sliding into debt that lasts for decades is really bad, you will be surprised to realize that most people underestimate their debts. If you sum up the total amount of credit card debts that people say they have and compare with the actual figures from credit card companies', a huge discrepancy of over $415 million is evident[9]. However, why the big discrepancy?

Many people rarely give the actual amount of debt they owe to avoid being embarrassed. However, denial about your credit status can escalate an already bad situation.

8. **With Commitment, it is Possible to Get out of**

---

[8] Digangi, C, 2015, *The Scary Link Between Credit Card Debt and Depression.* <available at> http://money.com/money/3848551/credit-card-debt-depression/

[9] Ibid

Debt. Though the problem of debt is distressful, it is possible to address it. When people appreciate that they are in debt and commit to overcoming the problem, it is possible to become debt free. Most successful people today were at some point entangled in financial debts.

The interesting thing about debt is that when you decide to tackle it, the lessons become very important in helping you grow financially. For example, lessons such as cutting unnecessary costs are used to help raise money even for other ventures such as personal investment.

Chapter Two: Examples of Debt and Why You Should Care

When you fall into debt, it creates a chain of problems that could affect every part of your life. In many cases, people tend to underestimate the impact of debts until it is too late. This chapter explores the impact of debts and why you should appreciate it and start caring. Additionally, it also outlines examples of debts.

Main Problems that can Result from Debt

When you are in debt, it becomes like a strong chain that makes you stall in the same position for many years. Because of the debts, most financial institutions will look at you as a high-risk party and decline applications for credit. This implies that you will also find it difficult to fund personal development.

In a couple of years, your close friends will be having big companies and growing them to the next level as you stagnate in the same place. Well, you cannot afford to continue hiding when you have debts. It is time to address them head-on and become successful. Here are additional reasons why you should care.

- Health Deterioration

If you take too long before paying your debt, your name will be forwarded to collection agencies that will go after you. The agencies will call regularly demanding that you pay the debt. In some cases, this could easily become a legal battle. The stress that comes with such demands could end up causing problems such as migraines and poor health.

- Damage to Your Credit Score

When you fall into debt, your credit score will drop drastically. Because the credit score is a measure of your creditworthiness, a poor score implies that no financial institution will agree to lend you money. Note that it is not just the financial organizations that are using credit scores today. You are also likely to get an application for phone credit and a mortgage declined.

As most lines of credit get closed, you will be left with few financial options such as payday loans that are very expensive. But these loans only risk sinking you deeper into debt. Note that in the event that you default on the payday loan, the interest rates could become higher plunging you deeper into debt.

Regrets

When you look at your current debt situation, one of the main problems will be regrets. You will start wondering what actually made you get into the problem of debt. This will grow from personal regrets to blaming other people such as your parents, close friends, and community.

- Strained Relationships

If you have a lot of debts, the chances are that your relationship will get strained. Debts impact financial related stress and can result in emotional and mental issues. Depending on how the debt accumulated, it could result to trust issues and even divorce. About 80% of couples who get divorced in the US indicate financial problems to be one of the primary causes[10].

- Low Productivity at Work

As the impact of debt becomes evident, the psychological effects are likely to be felt even at the workplace. You will feel odd as other people talk about their success stories with money and new ventures. To fit in their circles, you will be forced to create lies. This could culminate to self-guilt and more regrets. Ultimately, your productivity at work will take a downturn.

The main reason why you should care is that though you are in debt, it is not a permanent problem. This means that you

---

[10] CreditLoan, 2019, How Debt Affects Relationships and What to Do About It. <available at> https://www.creditloan.com/blog/how-debt-affects-relationships/

can still get out of it and reach your financial goals. But how do you do it?

You will only need to develop the right mindset and commit to clearing it. You will be surprised to know that a lot of people who are very successful today were at one point wallowing in debt. You can start by cutting off excesses in your lifestyle and directing the cash to clearing debts. You should also consider creating new lines of revenue to further attack the debt. With a clear plan, your debt can be erased!

Examples of Debts

1. A student loan of $30,000, requiring minimum repayment of $50 per month (Federal Direct Student Loan, interest 4%)

Standard loan repayment plans are considered the default status of most credits unless the terms and conditions indicate otherwise.

With the standard loan repayment of a $30,000 loan being $50, you might want to consider paying more to clear it within the stipulated time frame.

When this loan is offered at an interest rate of 4% and a repayment period of 120 months, the monthly payment would come to $304. Then, the total interest paid in the course of the entire repayment session would be $6,448 culminating to a total of $36,448.

2. A student loan of $30,000, requiring minimum repayment of $50 per month (Federal Direct Student Loan, 6% monthly interest)

When this loan is offered at an interest rate of 6%, the monthly repayment would come to $333. The total interest paid for the loan in the course of a 10 year period would come to $9,967. This would push the total loan repaid to $39,967.

The main difference between the total amount repayable in the first loan and the second one is $3,519 for the same period of 10 years. This means payment of an additional $29/ month. To pay the same total amount like the first loan, you would require paying a sum of $2,900 before the interest is applied.

3. A student loan of $30,000 (Income-based repayment, 4% interest rate, average monthly repayments on $47,000 per year)

It is important to note that income-based repayments (IBR) are only provided to graduates who qualify for them. The repayment takes a certain percentage of the learner's discretionary income to repay the credit. This means that the monthly income is dependent on how much you earn. If you are new, the rate is pegged at 10% but should not exceed ten years. Note that the median income for US college students is considered $47,000.

Therefore, if you take a $30,000 loan, the repayment will range from $245 and $304 every month. The total interest paid during a 10-year and 8-month period would be $7,141. This would bring the total payable amount to $37,141 by the time the entire loan is cleared.

Steve E. Carruso

Chapter Three: The Scary Psychology behind Impulse Spending

We have at one time or another fallen victim to impulse spending. Maybe you had simply taken a friend to the mall but ended up spending some money on a new dress. This happens because buying is an emotional process as opposed to a logical one.

This chapter is a closer evaluation of the psychology of impulse spending to demonstrate what it is and identify harmful spending patterns.

A Closer Look at the Psychology of Spending

Impulse buyers always look for items that will make them happy and elegant in front of others. This makes them easily fall prey to advertisements that promise ecstasy. However, the advertisements are designed as marketing strategies to capture the buyer's mind by shouting that the item on display is the best[11].

An impulse buyer may feel unhappy and believe that if they

---

[11] James, J, 2017, *Money, the Psychology of Money: Master Your Saving and Spending Habits*. New York: CreateSpace

Independent Publishing Platform.

wear expensive clothes, then they will get happiness and respect from peers. This perception motivates the impulse buyer to set out shopping in the market. When they get into the mall, a well-displayed item will catch their attention and they will draw closer to check it out.

At that point, they might remember another friend who uses a similar item. Thoughts of buying the item and going with it create ecstasy. At this point, they cannot resist the urge to buy. They buy the item without assessing whether it is too expensive or even comparing it with alternatives.

At the end of it all, impulse buying results in remorse and brings unhappiness that the buyers wanted to avoid. However, the process cannot be reversed and they will have to incur additional expense looking for the right item[12].

Factors that Fuel Impulse Spending

As shops invest more in marketing, buyers easily find themselves purchasing items they did not intend to buy. Here are some factors that influence impulse spending:

- **Fear of not finding the same item again**. Some people get overwhelmed when they enter a shop and get a customized item that no one else has. They end

---

[12] Ibid

up buying it so they can look unique with an item that is not available elsewhere in the market.

- **Fear of missing out.** When a new product is launched, it is possible to see a lot of people getting interested. This could make you to also order the same product. A good example is when Apple releases a new iPhone and the orders are too many to keep up with.

- **Money availability.** When a consumer has a lot of funds that are easily accessible when shopping, the probability of impulse spending is very high. This is the primary reason why a lot of people overspend on their credit cards.

- **Discounts and offers.** When a product that you have always desired to own has a discount attached to it, you could be tempted to purchase it even if you had not planned to.

- **Love for shopping.** There are people who derive pleasure in simply entering a mall and picking items. Such people will even look for more expensive stores that match their status, even when items sold there are more costly.

Identifying Harmful Spending Habits

In this part, I will list ten non-essential things that I bought, the reason for buying them, and then note the harmful spending patterns.

1. **iPhone X.** I bought the phone because of the hype it attracted all over the globe. I wanted to enjoy the new features such as the dual camera, stronger processor and the bliss of having the latest model.

2. **Nike shoes.** I liked the display of the shoes and ended up buying because I had cash readily available in the credit card. I was impressed by the fact that the shoe shouted that I will be a champion when wearing them. However, this was a marketing strategy for Nike and the seller.

3. **A new Lenovo laptop.** I bought this new laptop because most of my colleagues in the workplace were using Lenovo. However, my HP Laptop was still in good condition.

4. **Antique furniture.** I was motivated to buy this piece of furniture from the fact that it was drawn from the 19th Century. It was a special collection and I wanted to feel unique for being the only one with such furniture.

5. **New television.** The main motivation was that it was a smart television that could easily help me get online. However, I rarely used the feature because I did most of the online tasks on the laptop and smartphone.

6. **Kitchen cutlery.** I was moved by the impressive display of the cutlery in the shop. Though I had

purchased another set a few months earlier, I still ended up buying.

7. **New suit.** I went with my friend who was checking on his wedding suit, and I got carried away by the suit. It was interesting that the measurements perfectly suited me and I ended up buying with a credit card.

8. **A digital camera.** I like the idea holidaying in different parts of the world. When I found a Nikon camera with new specs, I was carried away. I imagined taking stunning early morning images on the great beaches of Hawaii or in Antarctica. I ended up buying the camera even though I still had another one that worked fine.

9. **Chandelier lamps.** While the lamps that I had at home were indeed great, the display and benefits that the marketer attached to the chandelier lamp made it irresistible. Indeed, I ended up spending more to have the lamps installed on the ceiling.

10. **Ice maker.** As a person who loves spending a lot of time outdoors, the idea of a great ice maker was very impressive. Though I had a smaller ice maker that served me well, I bought a new and bigger one because it was on discount.

After reviewing these non-essential items, I found a number of harmful spending patterns. First, my purchasing pattern was influenced by the attractive displays used in the store.

This made me buy items without carefully reviewing whether they would deliver value to me.

I also established that having readily available cash also made me desire to buy new items on display. This was a harmful pattern because I ended up buying new items even if the current ones were still functional.

Friends were also influencing me to purchase new items even when I had not planned to. This was wrong because I got carried away and rarely checked the overall quality of the item being purchased.

My desire to outdo others drove me to look for opportunities that elevated me from them. This is the main reason that made me crave for items on sale which made me stand out. However, this does not mean that the items were always of higher quality. For example, the 19th Century furniture I bought ended up breaking in a few months. I had to revert to my previous corner sofa. It was a total waste of money.

When I realized the dangers associated with impulse spending, I had to redefine my shopping behavior. It was one of the strategies that helped me become financially free. You can also avoid impulse buying by following the tips outlined in the next part.

How to Avoid Impulsive Spending

While the deals on different items might look irresistible, you can avoid impulse spending by ensuring you always shop with a list. This will help you to only pick the items that you need and had planned to buy. Here are other tips to help you avoid impulse spending:

- **Adopt a waiting period rule.** This is a very important strategy because it gives you ample time to review an item to ascertain whether you need it and it is of high value. A good waiting period should be at least 24 hours.

- **Always calculate the value of the item before purchasing it.** Because impulse buying is mainly emotional, you can stop it by being logical. One way of doing this is thinking about the time you would require to earn what the item costs. For example, if a suit is tagged $200, you will need about ten hours if you're earning $20 per hour. Therefore, is it worth buying? This way, your mind will tell you to walk away.

- **Reevaluate what you own.** Impulse spending often results in a loss of money because people rarely think about what they own. If you evaluate your current iPhone 7 that has been fantastic, you will realize that it is still great and you do not need a newer iPhone X.

- **Set shopping procedures.** If you want to reach

financial freedom faster, everything needs to follow a course. When it comes to shopping, it is important to follow three steps before buying any item. First, determine you need the item, then review the quality of the item, and finally compare the price with others in the market.

- **Use a no-spend challenge.** No spend challenges are periods when you cut purchases and do with what you have. During such periods, the no spend rules indicate that you can only buy a few basics such as toiletries while the rest of the money goes to savings.

- **Avoid shopping inside the mall.** If you order your products online and pick them at the storefront, you will reduce the danger of buying items simply because they have been displayed well on the shelf.

- **Unsubscribe from retail newsletters.** Many stores use newsletters to push offers and discounts to targeted clients. These can tempt you to spend more than you had planned. It is advisable to unsubscribe from such notifications and follow individual stores only when looking for offers.

- **Do not shop before reading reviews.** If you can take a closer look at an item that is very attractive, it will be easy to make the right decision whether to purchase or not. You can do this by reading feedback from past users to know about their experience after using the item under consideration. Reviews from experts can also help you to compare it to other similar items on the market.

- **Think about the last unplanned purchase that you regret.** Impulse spending always results in regrets. If you purchased an item without planning last time and regretted the decision, use it to avoid similar experiences in the future. Make sure to ask this question before making a purchase: "Will you end up regretting it like last time?"

- **Leave behind people who like impulse spending.** If you are a family person, it is important to leave out the members who can make you buy more than you had planned. For example, consider leaving your child behind when shopping in a mall because they could pick items that you had not intended to buy.

- **Seek expert help.** If you find that impulse spending is becoming too difficult to stop, consider seeking expert assistance. Professionals can help you to see the problem and develop creative ways to avoid unwanted purchases.

- **Do not purchase items that cannot be returned.** In many cases, items that have very low price tags are of poor quality and cannot be returned. This is very common with items on clearance sales.

Therefore, if a product does not have a money back guarantee, simply walk away even if the price is tempting or the display makes it irresistible.

- **Avoid taking extra cash when going shopping.** When many people have extra cash in their pocket or credit card, the temptation to overspend is very high. Therefore, you can avoid overspending if the cash available is only enough to purchase the items you planned to buy.

- **Change your friends.** If you have friends who love shopping and seeking to influence others' buying habits, it might be time to walk away. As you target reducing impulse purchases, consider searching for friends who share the same dream. Such friends will always encourage you to take no-spend challenges and other saving tips.

Steve E. Carruso

Chapter Four: How to Pay off Debt in 4 Easy Steps

Being in debt is a major burden that can hold back your life from success. You will realize that it is even worse because most debts, such as credit card loans, keep attracting severe penalties. Therefore, you will need to craft a way of clearing the debt.

The good news to you is that paying off the debts is not as complicated as you might have previously thought. This chapter will provide you with a complete guide on how to clear the debt. It focuses on creating the right mindset, rewarding yourself, and avoiding complicated budgeting procedures. The chapter also explains the 4-step debt eliminator method, shows you how to save on bank fees, and ends with a guide for a no-spend Challenge.

Creating the Right Mindset to Clear Your Debt

Getting the right mindset to tackle your debts is perhaps the first step in any march to financial freedom. Though it can take some time because society appears to encourage people to borrow and buy more, it is definitely worth it. If you find that the debt is starting to get out of control, simply drag it into the light and face the reality. Here is how to create the right mindset.

44

- Acknowledge the Debt

Today, many people do not admit that they are in debt. In some cases, you might not even be aware of the debt value because you have loans from multiple credit cards, bank, student loan and mortgage among others. Therefore, you need to acknowledge the debt and initiate own interventions before creditors start knocking.

You can do this by grabbing a notebook or opening a spreadsheet to list all the debts. How much do you owe in student loans, credit cards, car loans, and departmental stores among others? This will be the first step to creating a debt management plan[13].

- Accept your Debt and Move On

It is human to blame yourself about the current situation. Make sure to deal with emotions such as anger, regret, and guilt as opposed to sweeping them under the carpet. You could even consider seeking some help about the problem so that you start dealing with it.

What is more important is that you need to forgive yourself and move on. What made you fall into debt will become part

---

[13] Ramsey, D, 2013, The Total Money Makeover: A Proven Plan for Financial Fitness. London: Thomas Nelson

Steve E. Carruso

of the learning process so that you can avoid similar problems in the future. When you finally get out of debt, it will be a milestone. But you need to start somewhere.

- Get Motivation from Those Who Have Managed to Address Debts

When you are in debt, there is a tendency to think that your problem is unique. However, it is not. The reality is that many people have been in debt and managed to get out. These should be your source of motivation. For example, Richard managed to clear his $40,000 debt after developing the right mindset (Read more success stories of people who overcame debts later in this chapter).

- Come up with a Game Plan to Clear the Debt

After accepting that you are in debt and developing the desire to clear it, it is time to craft a game plan. This will be your strategy to steadily reduce the debt until it is eliminated completely. One of the components of your plan should be reducing spending in non-essential areas and directing the funds to clear the debt. You should also consider creating additional streams of revenue to help clear the debt faster.

- Reward Yourself when you Make every Milestone

To make the process of clearing debt fun, it is important to plan rewarding yourself. Do not see the process as a form of punishment. Just like a job promotion, you should reward every effort and milestone. For example, if you have a debt of $40,000, consider rewarding yourself with a token after clearing every $1,000, $5,000, and $10,000 respectively. This will help you to appreciate the current effort and offer additional motivation to keep moving on.

- Keep the Process as Simple as Possible

When you are trying to make things work or starting a long journey of repaying your debts, it is important to keep everything as simplified as possible. It is particularly important to avoid complicated budgeting procedures. Instead, you should consider using the standard budgeting spreadsheet to help you plan for the available revenue, what to pay for which loan, clear other expenses, track personal financial goals.

To track the entire process, consider setting reminders on your diary, computer, and phone. This will remind you when it is time to do the next budgeting, make some payment, or reward yourself after hitting a milestone.

The Four Step Debt Eliminator

No matter how big your debt appears, all that you need is a positive mind and a debt clearing strategy. This is why the 4-step debt eliminator strategy (commonly referred to as the debt snowball method) is recommended in most situations.

A Closer Look at the 4-Step Debt Eliminator Strategy

This debt eliminator method is aimed at motivating you to keep reducing the debt by attacking it, starting with the one that has the lowest amount. Once the smallest loan is knocked down, the amount that was used to repay it is directed to the subsequent small loan. The method works because of two things.

- You are able to pay a minimum amount required for all your loans. This implies that your credit cards, auto loans and other lines of credit will not add penalties that can increase the debt.
- By removing one debt after another, you can see some visible results. If you had initially thought that repaying debts is impossible, seeing a few of the loans drop off will provide a lot of motivation to clear the remaining amount[14].

How to use the 4-Step Debt Eliminator

This debt elimination method requires you to only follow

---

[14] Ramsey, D, 2013, The Total Money Makeover: A Proven Plan for Financial Fitness. London: Thomas Nelson

four simple steps to achieve financial freedom[15]. Take a look

- **Step 1: List your debts from smallest to largest regardless of interest rate.** Before deciding what to give more focus or what to anticipate, make sure to list all the debts. This should include their particulars such as the required minimum monthly repayment and time. The aim is to get all the balances in one place and compare with the available revenue before starting the repayment process.

- **Step 2: Make minimum payments on all your debts except the smallest.** By paying the minimum amount for all the loans except the smallest one, you will not get delinquent.

- **Step 3: Pay as much as possible on your smallest debt.** When you direct the remaining resources to attack the lowest debt, it implies that it will be cleared faster.

- **Step 4: Repeat until each debt is paid in full.** Now that the smallest debt is cleared, you will need to direct the effort to the next small loan until it is also cleared. In a few months or years, it will come as a surprise to realize that only one or a few loans will be remaining. You will also be highly motivated to clear

---

[15] Ibid

them faster.

- Sub-step – When you have multiple credit card loans, here are the main steps to follow.

  1. Make the minimum payment on all of your accounts

  2. Put as much extra money as possible toward the account with the highest interest rate

  3. Once that debt is paid off, start paying as much as you can on the account with the next highest interest rate. Repeat the cycle until all the credit card debts are paid

To demonstrate how the 4-step debt eliminator works, here is an example of John's debt.

- **Car Loan**: $20,000 at 6% with a monthly minimum repayment of $400.
- **Medical Loan**: $10,000 at 6.8% with a monthly minimum payment of $115;
- **Student Loan**: $5,000 at 6.8% with a monthly minimum payment of $60.

The required total minimum monthly repayment for John is $575. To clear the debt using the 4-step debt eliminator, John should plan to pay the minimum repayment amount for only the Car Loan and Medical Loan. This amounts to $515. Then, the rest of the finances should be directed at clearing the student loan.

Instead of only meeting the minimum repayment requirement for the Student Loan, John will attack it with more finances from his salary and other sources. For example, if he manages to pay $1000 for the student loan every month, it will take only five months to clear the smallest debt.

Once the Student Loan is cleared, the process should be repeated with the focus on the Medical Loan. This implies that the amount that John was using to clear the Student Loan should be directed at clearing the Medical Loan ($9,425 by the fifth month).

This process should be repeated until all the loans are cleared.

Useful Tips to Help Your Succeed when Using the Debt Eliminator

Though the debt eliminator method is easy to use, some people find it hard sticking to it and sometimes walk away when it is halfway. Here are some useful tips to use:

- **Look at the debt broadly, factoring all your sources of income.** As you list all the debts, it is also crucial to include all your sources of income. This will help you to understand the correct personal financial status and plan appropriately. For example, if you have a salary and a business that provides additional income, direct most of the resources towards clearing the debt.

- **Avoid falling back into debt.** In some cases, people have found themselves falling back into debt when the repayment burden eases. However, this could compromise the process you have taken a lot of time and resources to plan for. Instead of seeking debt, it is advisable to cut spending on non-essential items such as holidays and entertainment.

- **Plan for basic needs when using the debt eliminator.** One thing that you need to appreciate when trying to clear debt is that the basic needs have to be budgeted appropriately. For example, you should first deduct the money for rent, food, transport, kid's school fees, etc. before paying the loan.

- **Look for additional sources of income to clear the debt.** The primary target of using the debt eliminator method is to clear all the debts. Therefore, if you can make some additional income and direct it to knock off the debt, it will be cleared faster. Some great options include writing a book for sale on Amazon and blogging on your favorite topics.

- **Make sure to save for an emergency.** Even when making a lot of effort to clear the debt, an emergency can easily compromise everything. If your spouse falls ill and requires specialized medical attention, it is very easy to direct your funds there. To avoid such a scenario, it is important to have an emergency fund. As you plan for basic needs, some funds should also go to the emergency fund. It is also important to take medical insurance for the entire family.

How to Save on Bank Fees

One method you can use to save money using banks, is selecting the one with low-interest charges. If you take the monthly bank statement, you will be able to see how much fees were charged on the account. To cut this fee, here are some steps that you can use:

- Compare different banks' fees and switch to the one with lower charges
- Compare accounts and select the one with lower fees
- Avoid using another bank ATM to withdraw your money because it attracts additional charges
- Where possible, consider using digital channels because most of them are free or have very small charges
- Request bank statements by email as opposed to physical deliveries to avoid delivery-related fees
- Ensure you understand the monthly caps for your

accounts and ATM withdrawals to avoid additional charges

12 Ways to Save on Groceries

1. Stick to your Numbers when Shopping

Work on your grocery budget and stick to it. As you shop, have your calculator to ensure you stick to the budget. Here, the target is ensuring you understand the big picture of the financial debt to be cleared and attacking it bit-by-bit.

Remember that this will require you to shed off unnecessary content of your grocery list. For example, you can slash fast food from the list and stick to homemade, dried and crunchy fruits.

"We are under $80 a week for our family (two adults and a preschool kid). We have done away with pizzas. You can also do it and make a significant saving to help cut your debt."

2. Check your Store First

Before you set off buying new groceries, it is important to check the pantry for an alternative. That is right! Simply because you are out of one item does not imply you must head to the market. The chances are that you have an alternative that can be used.

If you like having a pineapple cocktail every evening, you can opt to do with the mangoes or apples because they are the options available in the fridge. Other substitutes you can use include preparing popcorns instead of rushing to the market for new cashew nuts.

"The idea behind using substitutes is that alternative food sources such as nuts, fruits, veggies, and meat provide the body with more minerals and nutrients. I'm on the second week and have managed to knock $231 by using substitutes."

3. It is Time to Start Storing your Meals

Preparing a meal costs so much! But you can cut this cost by a huge margin by preparing large meals and freezing the leftovers. Nothing beats already having it in the freezer.

Think of the effort, materials, and costs that go into preparing a meal. By preparing a big meal, you can save on energy and food materials such as spices that would have been used to prepare several meals.

"At first I found it hard to notice the impact. However, I established that my food reserves were going for longer as the power bill shot down. After comparing last month and others, I managed to save $209."

4. Round up your Grocery Estimates

Keeping track of your grocery expenses helps to ensure you are on top of the budget all the time. However, there are times when the cost of items does not match with your estimates. For example, the price of an item on your budget list could be $5.26. To avoid getting surprises, it is advisable to round up the cost to full figures.

"Rounding the price to complete figures such as $5.26 to $6.0 means that your budget will always cover the listed items. I regularly check the price of different items on the list especially when budgeting to ensure I make the estimates as precise as possible."

5. Utilize the Scan it Feature

After budgeting, the main question remains; "How do you operate within the boundaries of the defined limit?" Most grocery stores today have a 'Scan It' feature that allows you to walk around and scan items on sale as you shop.

Scanning the items helps you follow the totals to avoid getting surprised. The Scan It feature also helps you to decide whether some items that you had selected are really necessary.

"I like the Scan It feature because it helps me to check alternatives that I can pick at the same or lower price. Instead of queen cakes, the Scan It feature helps me to pick alternatives such as donuts."

6. Work and Stick to Your Meal Plan

When planning for meals, factor the offers from a specific store. For example, a store that has opened new offers on an item of interest is a great place to get your purchases. Then, buy in large quantities and freeze the supplies. Try to avoid shopping when hungry because you are likely to impulse buy the items on the shelf.

"By planning meals well, I am able to evaluate the nutrient needs and even negotiate for lower rates. On average I am able to save about 10% by sticking to the meal plan and pitching a tent on stores releasing new discounts."

7. Only Buy what you Need

Many are the times when you will get tempted to buy an item because it is discounted. Though that item is marked one for $5 and four for $10, it does not mean that you have to buy it. The chances are that you will end with a surplus going into waste.

"I always work with what I need. First I draw a plan of what to buy and only pick such offers when they fall within the budgetary limits. For example, if I had planned to buy an item for $5 but the store has an offer of two for $5, it is okay."

8. Shop Online as Opposed to Visiting the Mall

When you walk into a mall, the temptation to pick more

items from the shelves is at times irresistible. But there is a way out. You can purchase the items of interest online instead of visiting the mall.

"After realizing this secret and its potential to help build savings, I advised my wife to always prepare a list of all the items we need. Then, we order them online and drive to the store to pick them up. This way, we are able to save time and avoid walking into the store. It is also convenient for us because we have little kids."

9. Plan to Eat Dinner Leftovers for Lunch

The common practice in many homes is preparing a nice dinner and taking lunch in a restaurant or hotel. For others, both dinner and lunch are bought from cafes. This can raise your overall cost of food with a great margin. Here is a way out.

Instead of going to a café, consider preparing a great dinner every night and using the leftovers for lunch. This means that you can enjoy more nutritious foods and save the money that could have gone to buy the food.

"Because my husband and I work near our living house, lunches for Monday to Thursday are taken from supper leftovers. We have saved more than $1200 since we started the plan."

10. Buy Generic

If you take a closer look at the leading sellers in the market today, their products have a very high price tag. In most of the cases, these stores want to attract a specific type of clientele. However, most of the food they sell is junk and unhealthy.

"To make some savings, we shop at the grocery stores that have made a name for low price products and focus on buying generic stuff. We have cut junk such as pizzas from our budget that helps save about $250 while generic stuff further cuts about $250 per month.

11. Only Buy Meat when on Sale

Meat can be expensive depending on the preferred choice. For example, boneless skinless chicken thighs are cheaper compared to chicken breasts. To keep the cost of proteins low, you could also consider alternatives such as legumes that are also delicious.

"At home, my wife and I are always on the lookout for the stores have an offer on meat. The good thing is that the offers are announced every few days by different stores. Besides, we have also subscribed to the stores for notifications when such offers are announced. This way, we are able to save between $250 and $350 every month."

12. Do Not go Shopping with Over-spenders

If you want to save on groceries, the over-spenders should always be left behind. In many cases, they insist that you add more items even though it was not included in the list. For example, the attractive display of oranges and pineapples can easily make over-spenders add them to the shopping cart though the target item was passion fruits.

"In my family, the over-spender is my husband. He can end up filling the shopping cart even when the aim was picking only a packet of milk. By leaving him behind when am going to the grocery store helps me save an average of $400 per month."

Debt Success Stories

No matter your debt situation, the reality is that you can overcome it. Here are some debt success stories you should read:

1. Richard, a Biologist Cleared $40,000 Debt

When speaking to frugality magazine called *The Disease Called Debt*, Richard revealed that his debt problem started with the higher education loan. Then, he slid further into $40,000 debt after taking an auto loan and a series of credit card loans[16].

Richard's ability to overcome the debt was made possible by his commitment. He indicates that he tried with a number of methods until he got the one that worked in his situation.

Living without debt for Richard helps him to enjoy life and become more productive. He indicates that when he was in debt, his hands and indeed life were tied so that it was impossible to reach full potential. Now, he can afford a vacation and enjoy good times with family without worrying about a nagging debt problem.

Richard explains that his health has also improved. Unlike during the time when he was in debt, he can now afford to relax, do more exercises, and spend more time with the family. All of these have reduced problems such as migraines that were initially common to him.

Richard emphasizes that the biggest thing that bogged him down when he was in debt were thoughts about how to overcome it. However, he advises people to appreciate the problem and take it head-on.

2. Heron Abegaze and Elijah Bankole Paid Thousands of

[16] Disease called Debt, 2018, *Debt Success Stories: Richard Paid off $40,000 in Debt.* <Available at>https://diseasecalleddebt.com/debt-success-stories-richard/

Debt in Just Three Years

Attacking debt and knocking it down is possible if you evaluate your life and target the areas where you can slash spending. This is the trick that Abegaze and Bankole used to clear off nearly $162,000 of debt. The couple attacked the debt with savings raised by declining friends' invitations, postponing holiday, and foregoing fancy cars[17].

For the couple, there is nothing as enjoyable as relaxing on a weekend with a spouse without worrying about the debt burden. It makes life foggy and could even wreck a relationship. Today, Abegaze and Bankole recite their journey with enthusiasm about the strength of their bonds.

The couple has also learned about the importance of transparency and communication in a relationship. As a couple, knowing about the status of the debt and love for each other made them combine synergies and clear it together. If Bankole was alone, the journey could probably have taken longer.

However, the most important thing that Bankole insists about the entire journey is the lessons they have learned.

---

[17] Judith,O, 2018, *How this Couple Paid Off Nearly $162,000 Of Debt In 3 Years*. <Available at > https://www.refinery29.com/en-us/2018/03/194339/how-one-couple-paid-off-all-their-debt

They have come to appreciate that there is nothing that one cannot do with correct planning. The tricks used to save the money have helped the couple to also become successful in their investments.

3. Melanie Lockert Cleared her $81,000 Student Loan

Back in 2013, Lockert had a student loan of about $81,000. But the scary thing about it was that she was unable to find steady work that could help her to pay the loan faster. Therefore, she ventured into the pool of self-employment and started blogging to try and get money for sustenance and repaying the loan[18].

The effort paid off when her income tripled what she was earning when employed. To clear the debt, she set a target and budgeted well to prioritize the student loan. She managed to clear her debt earlier than one year.

Since breaking away from debt, Lockert has shifted to her dream city, Los Angeles, where she still runs her blog. She indicates that the freedom she has earned has helped her change perspective in life. Unlike in the past, there is nothing that she cannot achieve with proper planning and budgeting.

---

[18] Adam, H, *21+ Motivational Stories About Getting out of Debt.* <available at> https://adamhagerman.com/21-get-out-of-debt-stories/

For Lockert, the idea of being able to fully control finances has ushered in a new beginning. She sees the debt era as a crucial learning phase that simply prepared her for bigger roles in the society. This is why she says that her life and success are only getting started and the world of opportunities is fully open for her. It is a new dawn.

4. Jackie Beck and Her Husband Paid Over $152,000

Beck and her husband found themselves with a debt problem of $152,000 that included a mortgage. However, about $52,000 was consumer debt that largely came from their credit cards. To clear the debt, Beck and her husband planned to attack it by first creating an emergency fund[19].

By attacking the debt together, it was possible to clear it faster and start enjoying financial freedom. But the couple indicates that this revealed their hidden potential to achieve greater things. They have started exploring new areas of investment and target being equally successful by applying the same strategies.

As a couple, clearing the debt together has helped them understand the love they have for each other. The debt was seen as the dark moments in their lives. By sticking together,

---

[19]Adam, H, *21+ Motivational Stories About Getting out of Debt*. <available at> https://adamhagerman.com/21-get-out-of-debt-stories/

they now believe that nothing can come between them no matter how complicated it is.

Waking up every morning and taking your breakfast without worrying that a recovery agency is on your back or a bank will come knocking is a great achievement for Beck. She indicates that they have found new happiness because it is now possible to take more time together, love more, and grow together.

Beck says that she has also learned the tricks of falling into success; planning for everything. She indicates that her family no longer spends what it does not have because it is the roadmap to debts.

5. Deacon Hayes Paid off $52,000 in 18 Months

For Deacon and his wife, being in debt was a major cause of family strain. However, he believed that it was possible to clear it and live a happy life. He started by selling off unnecessary stuff including his car to clear the loan. Now, he is working on clearing the mortgage in ten years.

As a couple, Hayes points out that being bound by chains of debt is dangerous. Most of the debts, especially those based on credit cards, keep growing and you might end up dying in debt. But Hayes discovered the secret of commitment and persistence in clearing debts[20].

Today, Hayes explains that he has found new freedom because he can enjoy every moment of their lives without someone calling to bother them about debts. They no longer fear that they can be denied more credit to advance their business because of poor credit score. It is truly a free world!

When Hayes talks about the journey to financial freedom, he always insists on the importance of having support from loved ones. As he sold off his car and started a frugal lifestyle, he had the support and love from his wife. Taking the journey together makes it easy even when the going gets tough.

---

[20]Adam, H, *21+ Motivational Stories About Getting out of Debt.* <available at> https://adamhagerman.com/21-get-out-of-debt-stories/

Chapter Five: How to Do a "No Spend Challenge"

If you want to save more money to pay debts or build your portfolio, a No Spend Challenge might be the right option for you. At first, many people ask; "How can one stay without spending?" Well, if you are surprised, I had initially also thought it was an uphill task until I tried it.

A No Spend Challenge is a great method to jump-start big savings goals or even knock off the last part of a nagging debt. More importantly, when you stop spending over a period of time, it is a learning session to help you break shopping addiction, avoid living from paycheck to paycheck, and opening your world of opportunities. You will learn that nothing in life is impossible through planning and commitment.

This chapter is a comprehensive guide on how to do a No Spend challenge. It helps you to pick the right time-frame, select the allowances, and finally outlines useful tips to help you succeed in the challenge.

How to Do a No Spend Challenge

The first thing you need to do is deciding the type of No Spend challenge that you want to do. Here, you will need to

Steve E. Carruso

set two important components; Allowances and Time Frame.

1. Select the Allowances

Allowances in a No Spend challenge is the amount that you are allowed to spend. At this point, you might need to go back and define the difference between a *want* and *need*. For example, if you take the case of a *need* such as food, you might want to narrow down to groceries only or *groceries* and some *restaurants* on special occasions[21].

Other examples of needs that should be included in the allowance include medical products, toiletries, and gas. Note that when you list an item such as toiletries, it is important to be specific. For example, you are allowed to spend on toilet paper.

The primary target is ensuring you create a complete list of needs for reference during the challenge. This will help you to know what you are allowed to spend on and what is forbidden.

2. Select the No Spend Time-frame

There are many no spend time-frames you can select. However, you are encouraged to start from the shorter time-

---

Ramsey, D, 2013, The Total Money Makeover: A Proven Plan for Financial Fitness. London: Thomas Nelson

frames and work your way up. Here are the main time-frames to consider:

- ***No Spend Day Challenge***

The No Spend day challenge is an ideal point for starters who want to test how much they can save before making a decision to advance to longer time-frames. Because it only focuses on a single day, the focus is limited to only a few activities. However, they could have a great impact on helping clear debts or build savings.

1. Look for free entertainment events instead of paying for them
2. Consider cooking at home as opposed to eating in a restaurant
3. Walk or cycle around instead of using the family car
4. Take time to explain the challenge to the family members and bond together. Their support will be very important especially when you start taking longer No Spend time frames.

Before you can move on to the next challenge, it is advisable to repeat the No Spend day challenge for a number of times. Remember to carefully review how much you saved during the challenge as a motivation.

Steve E. Carruso

- ***No Spend Week Challenge***

When you decide to take this challenge, it is important to have a clear list of things you do on the specified week. Here are some of the main activities that you should consider for the No Spend week challenge.

1. Consider preparing weekly meals and using them without going to a restaurant. However, if your allowance allows you to spend in a restaurant, consider limiting the amount to spend there

2. Make sure to prepare coffee or tea at the workplace instead of rushing to the restaurant during the breaks. If your workplace does not allow you to prepare beverages, carry some from home

3. Instead of paying for a fitness club, consider walking or engaging in activities that bring together family and friends. For example, you can plan to walk with friends or cycle in the evening with other family members

4. Because you have a whole week to cut spending, it is time to do some chores that would otherwise require hiring someone. Good examples include washing your car and cleaning the carpet

5. Consider reading free books on the open library, Library of Congress, and internet archives as opposed to paid libraries.

6. It is also important to get involved in family fun activities such as painting that can help you achieve the main goal of not spending in the week

The same way you reviewed the No Spend day challenge, it is important to repeat for the weekly challenge. This will demonstrate the progress you are making and help motivate you to try longer No Spend periods.

- ***No Spend Month Challenge***

When you repeat the No Spend week challenges, a habit of spending on what is important and leaving non-important components out will start developing. As you start the No Spend month challenge, you will be asking the question: "Is this item really necessary?"

You will learn to get satisfied with the items you have and focusing on getting the best from them. Here are some key activities to consider during the No Spend month challenge:

1. Consider taking more time with the family as opposed to leaving for holiday. This will help you cut the cost of the flight, camping, and all the foods you would have eaten during the holiday. Instead, you can have great times with the family in the backyard.
2. Prepare do-it-yourself gifts for the family instead of buying them from the store. This activity will make

the family more engaged and strengthen your bonds.

3. Plan to do common repairs on the house instead of calling a technician. The good thing is that you can easily follow video guides on repairing house parts such as roofing or wall painting.

4. During the week, consider using public transport or riding to work. This will help to promote your physical fitness as you continue saving money.

5. On entertainment, consider subscribing to free video channels as opposed to visiting the theaters. This will also help you to take more time with the family.

What to Do after a No Spend Challenge

It is important to appreciate that No Spend challenges can be difficult especially if are getting started. When you go through a challenge, it is prudent to pat yourself on the back. You have made it! But before reverting to the older ways, it is important to also do the following:

1. Establish how much money you have saved during the challenge. It is important to be specific and ensure that the funds are directed to a specific course. For example, you can use the funds to reduce debts, build savings, or enlarge the emergency funds.

2. What did you learn during the No Spend period? Though the primary goal of the challenge was to save

money, there will be a lot to learn along the way. For example, you will learn that involving your spouse and the entire family to tackle a challenge makes the process easy.

3. Establish the obstacles that you want to conquer during the next challenge. Though you were determined to stick to the No Spend plan, some challenges such as festivities might have made it difficult to complete the entire challenge. Draw measures to address these difficulties.

4. Establish when the next challenge should be. Though you thought that raising $1000 to repay a debt is hard, the No Spend challenge has helped you to raise more! Such motivation will make you look forward to the next challenge. Remember that if the weekly challenge was a success, it is advisable to go for a monthly challenge. Indeed, you could even extend it to a few months.

Sit down with a pen and paper to look at the bigger picture of the No Spend idea. For example, if you take a $30 lunch every day, think of the amount that will be saved if you save that for 100 days (about three months). It will be $30*100=$3000. This is the motivation you need to keep moving on with the challenges.

Tips for Successful No Spend Challenge execution

While the calculations of how much you will save during the challenge can be impressive, it is important to appreciate that some people end up failing midway. These are useful tips to help make your No Spend challenge successful.

1. Start By Determining Why You Want To Undertake the Challenge

To successfully complete a No Spend challenge, it is important to establish why you are doing it. This becomes the driving factor to help you overcome the urge to rush to the theaters or do away with a holiday for a simple home movie. The goal could be building your savings or reducing your debt.

2. Set the Rules of The No Spend Challenge

Creating some rules will act like a boundary that tells you do not go beyond a specific point. The rules include things such as the allowances, the time-frame, what not to eat and places to avoid. To ensure that the rules are implemented, it is important to put them at a point where they are easily accessible. For example, display them on your living room wall, desktop, and even phone.

3. Discuss the Challenge with Family and Friends

It is important to point out that if you lack support from those close to you, the chances are that the challenge will not be successful. The family is especially crucial to helping you avoid excesses and optimize savings during the No Spend period.

If you have a spouse, they can help you especially in identifying alternatives as opposed to rushing to the grocery store when an item is out. Because your friends and family members want you to succeed, they will stick around to ensure you do.

4. Get Creative with what you have

If you take a closer look at your home, there are many ways of cutting cost by simply getting creative. For example, the beans in the store can be a great source of proteins instead of buying meat every other day. You can also prepare gift cards and use them for a family event as opposed to buying new things.

5. Remove Distractions that Encourage Shopping

As you start the No Spend challenge, it is important to appreciate that temptations to shop will still come your way. Therefore, you should avoid anything that encourages shopping. For example, you should unsubscribe to emails that regularly shout new deals on offer by a local store.

Steve E. Carruso

The time you take shopping should also be replaced with alternative tasks. For example, instead of going shopping on a Sunday afternoon, consider spending time with your family and playing games such as chess or watching movies. It can also be a great time to read a book or learn new skills.

6. Hide Credit Cards

When you go to buy an item during the No Spend period, having a credit card can encourage impulse buying. However, keeping the credit card away and only taking enough cash for specific items helps you to remain on course to optimize savings.

7. Engage in a Money Making Activity

Even as you put a lot of focus on cutting cost, it is advisable to also consider creating new streams of revenue. This will go a long way in helping to increase savings. Some good money making ventures include blogging, writing content for websites, selling photography, or part-time work in your area of specialization.

In some cases, people have started part-time money making ventures only for it to become their full-time work. For example, if you are an expert in a specific area such as health, vehicle mechanics, or agriculture, you could consider running a related blog.

8. Look for Motivation from People who have done No Spend challenges

Even if you are motivated by the primary goal of optimizing savings, it is also advisable to look at other people who have been successful. This will motivate you to also become successful. You can learn more tips for No Spend challenges and even new financial management skills.

Steve E. Carruso

Part Two: Building Wealth

Chapter Six: How to Automate Your Finances

If you take a closer look at your finances, the number of things that you are required to do can be overwhelming. You are required to prepare monthly budgets, remit money to repay loans, prepare financial accounts and many others. Is it possible to articulately manage all the tasks? The answer is "yes" when you use the right automation.

This chapter is a closer look at automation to help you manage your finances more prudently. It demonstrates why you need an emergency fund and further explores the leading financial app automation app, Mint.

Why you need an Emergency Fund

According to Murphy's law, "anything that can go wrong will go wrong". This means that even if you have taken the right measures to prevent accidents or bad occurrences, it is impossible to be 100% secure[22].

A company can go under. Employees can get laid off. Freelance work can be hard to get at some period. You can get sick. Bad things happen! Therefore, how do you deal with such situations? You need an emergency fund to help see you through the difficult period.

The need for an emergency fund is more important in today's professional climate than any other time in the past because the old model where people used to start working at 20 years of age and exiting at 55 years is no longer applicable[23]. Some people secure employment when they are well beyond 30 while others have only known contractual jobs.

How to Build an Emergency Fund

One thing that you need to know is that building an emergency fund cannot be done overnight. It requires commitment and a proper strategy. Here is an account of how to create an emergency fund.

1. **Set the long term emergency fund goal:** If you do not have a clear goal, it will be difficult to know

---

[22] Chatterjee, A, 2016, Is the statement of Murphy's Law valid? *Complexity*, 21 (6): 374–380.

[23] IbID

where you are headed. You should create an emergency savings account, and then set meaningful and achievable goals[24]. The best thing is to budget for the emergency fund as you do for the loan and other needs.

2. **Build one month worth of savings in the emergency fund:** Look at the emergency fund through the lens of "What would happen if I lose my job today?" or "What would I do if a major financial emergency hits my family?" After saving funds worth one month of living, you have to move to the next level of growing it.

3. **Divide the additional cash you generate between savings and debt:** Whether you generate additional cash from a No Spend month or a new stream of revenue, make sure to divide the funds between the debt and emergency funds. If you are using the Snowball's 4-step debt eliminator, consider increasing the amount of funds going into emergency funds after knocking down the smallest loans.

4. **Take advantage of your employer's emergency funding:** If your employer provides an emergency cover, it means that you have a right to it. This means

---

[24] Ramsey, D, 2013, The Total Money Makeover: A Proven Plan for Financial Fitness. London: Thomas Nelson

that you will not need to use your own emergency fund in case of a medical emergency because it is already covered.

5. **Avoid drawing funds from your emergency cover unless it is necessary:** As the name suggests, the emergency funds should only be used when unexpected events happen. Therefore, it should not be easy to reach the cash for regular shopping or even going on a holiday. If you want to raise money for holiday, consider saving it or tapping what is coming from passive income lines.

Apps you can use for financial automation

Financial automation has become the ultimate method to help people complete financial tasks, know the areas to slash spending, pay debts, and grow faster to financial freedom. One app that has stood out in the market because of its efficiency in financial automation is Mint. Here is a closer look at the app.

Mint

Mint is one of the leading finance automation applications designed to help you control all finances in one place. It is a free online service with over 15 million users across the globe. It only takes a few seconds to sign up and allows you to add multiple financial accounts to follow.

When you complete setting up the app, it downloads your financial data. It also downloads it every moment you visit[25].

The Mint dashboard allows you to do things like budgeting, set financial goals, and pools all the financial accounts in one place.

The Main Features of Mint

- **Budgeting and Tracking Expenses:** This is the primary feature of the application. It allows you to budget finances and further tracks the expenses to help you achieve personal financial goals.

To use the app for budgeting, simply navigate to the auto-categorization section to access the predefined categories for keying in budget items. It also allows you to create your own categories if the available templates are not impressive.

- **Creating and Managing Goals:** This feature is used to set and track goals. For example, you can set goals such as paying your debt or saving for a new home. The goals will be reflected in your monthly budget.

---

[25] Jim, W, 2019, *Best Personal Finance Software apps of 2019.* <available at> https://wallethacks.com/best-personal-finance-software-apps/

- **Monitoring Own Credit Score:** This feature allows you to track the entire financial picture and present them by simply clicking the "Show Details" button. The feature shows important components of your credit rating such as the credit score, the age of credit accounts, payment history.

- **Prompt alerts:** When you get mint, it sends prompt notifications so that you can take timely actions. The app will notify you if you go over budget in a specific category, fall late with fees, or plan large purchases. It also reminds you when to pay bills.

One thing that makes Mint stand out from others is that it integrates with your mobile phone to ensure that you will never miss an alert or warning even when away. Besides, it also sends weekly reviews that you can use to carry further personal financial analysis with more advanced software or a financial expert.Why try to remember everything when automation software can help? Consider trying Mint.

Chapter Seven: Investing for Absolute Beginners

If you want to become successful, you have to invest. Investment provides you with an opportunity to grow and become the millionaire you have always imagined. However, investing can be scary because of the risks along the way. But you should not be scared because there is nothing that is risk-free.

This chapter provides beginners with useful insights on how to invest. It demonstrates how most successful people succeed in their investments and digs deeper into three main investment options; 401k (plus company match), Roth IRA, and Mutual Funds. Finally, it demonstrates why investment in housing returns 0% after inflation.

How Regular Folks Become Millionaires

Every time that the list of top billionaires in the globe hits the headlines, you are left with one question on the mind: "How did they make it?" However, a closer look at where most of them started reveals that they were ordinary folks who dared to dream and created a pathway to success. You too can become the next millionaire by following the strategies that they followed.

1. **Develop the right mindset:** Investment is all about the mindset. When you decide to invest and become successful, all the energies are directed there so that nothing will stand in the way. Do not let the risks that lay on the way misguide you. Make a decision and follow it to become successful.

2. **Learn from those who are already successful:** To curve your way to becoming successful in life, it is important to look at those who are already successful. This way, you can learn the methods they used and note the mistakes they made so that you can avoid them. Interestingly, you will find that some top minds such as Google and Apple founders started in a garage or in very difficult situations. Well, you can also make it.

3. **You do not have to start big to become a successful investor:** One misconception that some people hold is that you require a lot of money to start investing. The little you have is enough to start investing. If the investment portfolio of interest requires more, you can generate it by doing away with the non-essential things at home. For example, you could sell a high-end car, buy a smaller vehicle for the family, and commit the extra funds to invest.

4. **Explore the best investment opportunities:** If you can identify good investment opportunities, rest

assured that you'll enjoy impressive returns. Here, you should think of ventures that pay high returns such as mutual funds. Before you can venture into the selected investment option, make sure to carry comprehensive research about its operations and to develop the right expectations.

5. **Focus on creating multiple streams of revenue:** After commencing your investment, you have to keep working on new ventures. This will finally create multiple streams of revenue and catapult you into financial freedom.

When it comes to investing, there is no obstacle standing between you and success. Now is your time. Get out and grab that opportunity to become a millionaire!

Introduction to Compound Interest

Compound interest rate is a very useful tool when it comes to investment and saving. Whether you are saving money in a long term investment plan or an emergency fund, the accumulation of compound interest helps to boost returns.

Compound interest is the interest that is calculated on both the saved principle and accruing interest. It is calculated by multiplying the initial principle by one plus annual interest raised to the number of compound periods minus one (see

86

the formula below)[26].

$A = P (1 + r/n)^{(nt)}$.

A = the future value of the investment/loan (it includes interest)
P = the principal investment amount or the initial deposit/loan

r = the annual interest rate (decimal)
n = the number of times that interest is compounded annually
t = the number of years the money is borrowed or invested for

NOTE: The above formula provides the actual value of an investment in the future, which is inclusive of compound interest + principle. Therefore, if you wish to narrow down to only compound interest rate, use the formula below[27].

Total compounded interest = $P (1 + r/n)^{(nt)} - P$

Compound Interest Impact on Investment

When your investment return is based on compound

---

[26] Previte, J, and Hoffman, R, 2014, *Essential Financial Mathematics*. Washington: Lulu.com

[27] Ibid

interest, your portfolio will grow rapidly because the interest is calculated on both the principle and the accrued interest. For example, if you put $100 into a saving scheme that has compounded interest rate of 10%, it will be worth $110 by the end of the first year. However, if it stays there for another year, the new principle will be $110. Therefore, the p by the close of the second year will be $21 and the total principle $121.

Take another example of a person who joins a mutual fund offering 7% compounded interest rate annually. If the account will have saved $1 million in 20 years, the new principle will have grown to $3.87 million.

401K (Plus Company match)

Employer matching your 401K (retirement contribution) implies that the employer is contributing a specific amount towards your retirement saving plan. The contribution by the employer is dependent on the amount of your annual contribution[28].

Based on the conditions set by your employer's 401K plan, the contribution that you make could be matched by using

---

[28] Claire, B, 2019, *How 401K Matching Works.* <available at>https://www.investopedia.com/articles/personal-finance/112315/how-401k-matching-works.asp

different methods. The common method is where the employer matches the percentage that the employee makes to the 401K plan up to a specific amount of your salary.

The employer may also opt to match your contribution up to a certain dollar quantity. This matching is done irrespective of the compensation you get.

Why Match Your 401K Contribution?

It is important to appreciate that the conditions of the 401K plan differ widely depending on the employer. Other than the standard requirement for contribution and withdrawal as required under the Employee Retirement Income Security Act (ERISA), your employer is free to set the conditions for 401k[29].

The employer could opt to use a generous method or a more stringent one. No matter the method that the employer uses, you have to appreciate that it is free money topped on your retirement benefit savings. Therefore, make sure to grab it!

How the Matching Operates

Assume that your employer is making a 100% match on the

_____

[29] Claire, B, 2019, *How 401K Matching Works.* <available at>https://www.investopedia.com/articles/personal-finance/112315/how-401k-matching-works.asp

contribution that you make annually, to a maximum of 3% annual income. If your salary is $60,000 per year, the employer will contribute $1,800. You will also be required to contribute $1,800 to the retirement plan in order to get the marching benefit.

A more common marching scheme preferred by employers is the model that offers 50% matches of employee contribution that equals 6% of the yearly earning. This means that if your annual salary is $60,000, the employer is eligible to contribute $3,600 for marching. But he will only contribute $1,800 because the marching benefit is capped at 50%. In this case, you will be required to contribute $3,600 in order to get full employer matching benefit.

The Contribution Limits

Irrespective of whether the payments to your 401k plan are being done by you or employer matching, the deferrals have to follow the annual contribution limit set by the Internal Revenue Service (IRS). For example, the contributions by employers in 2019 to all 401k accounts of the same employees were capped at 56,000 or 100% compensation (whichever comes first).

In the case of elective salary deferrals that are paid by the employees, the limit is capped at $19,000[30].

NOTE: The sum of employer matches does not count towards the employee's deferral limit. Also, you should appreciate that the limits could be updated every year (commonly done around October -November).

Vesting

Besides regularly reviewing your 401K matching needs, it is also prudent to check on vesting schedules. This schedule dictates the level of ownership for employees to the employer's contribution depending on the number of years of employment.

Even if the employer has a very attractive matching plan; you might be required to forego some or all contribution in the event of job termination. A common schedule allows you a percentage of the employer's contribution that increases with your tenure. The Bureau of Labor a Statistics gives five years for you to be fully vested.

The Roth IRA – Your secret retirement weapon

Roth IRA is a unique retirement account that provides tax benefits such as tax-free growth of personal investment.

---

[30] Ibid

However, not all people qualify for this investment.

Roth IRA encourages people to save progressively by providing tax-related benefits. Unlike the preceding scheme that used to tax investors' savings, money in the Roth IRS plan is tax-free. This implies that the Roth IRA withdrawal that you make later in retirement will be tax-free[35].

The Roth IRA is considered an account that holds the investors' funds as opposed to investment itself. The accounts are opened through brokers and you will be required to select where you want your funds to be directed to. The main options include exchange-traded funds (ETFs), bonds, socks, and mutual funds.

Are You Eligible for Roth IRA?

One thing that you will find vexing about Roth IRA is that you will not be eligible if your income is high. Starting from 2019, the rules of investing in Roth IRA were changed. Now, the amount that you can contribute to Roth IRA starts to shrink when it hits certain thresholds that are adjusted based on your growing income. For example, the maximum contribution of a married couple is $6,000[31]. The contribution continues to shrink as the income rises until

---

[31] iBid

you reach a point and it is halted.

It is also important to note that you can only contribute earned income. This means the income that you earn from being employed or even self-employed. If you get income such as scholarship and fellowship that is taxable, you are also eligible for the Roth IRA.

Other types of income that can allow you to make savings at Roth IRA include taxable differential and military alimony[32].

The earned incomes that cannot be used on the Roth IRA include dividends and interests from other investments, rental property, and revenue from pension schemes. Besides, you will not be allowed to include other types of income like IRA distributions, K-1 income, and Social Security.

Major Benefits of Joining Roth IRA

As an investor, the primary focus should be opportunities that allow you to optimize profits. One way of achieving this is picking opportunities like Roth IRA where your investment is tax-free. Here are other benefits to expect when you start saving in this scheme.

- The amount you contribute does not follow the

---

[32] Ibid

common minimum distribution model that is used by
401K starting at the age of 70½. This implies that
Roth IRA can be effectively used to optimize returns
and pass them to beneficiaries[33].

- When you decide to withdraw Roth IRA scheme, no
tax or penalty is imposed. The underlying principle of
the scheme is that the income that you are using had
already been taxed before being directed to the Roth
IRA.

- When you reach year 59½, Roth IRA allows you to
take away all the contribution including earnings
therein. Note that no federal taxes are levied. This is a
great boost for people who are starting or entering
retirement.

- The Roth IRA money can be used to pay for college
expenses without attracting a penalty. This is very
helpful in making your college life smooth[34].

- The plan allows people of all ages to participate. As
long as you have income that is allowed on the Roth
IRA and you pay taxes, it is a great point to start
building your savings.

---

[33]   RothIRA.co.m,   2019,   *Roth   IRA   Limits.*   <available   at>
https://www.rothira.com/roth-ira-limits

[34] Ibid

Mutual funds and ETFs

Mutual funds and Exchange traded funds (ETFs) are funds that consist of different types of assets and present investors with a great way of diversifying their portfolios. They are created from pool fund investing that is designed to help investors enjoy economies of scale. They also allow managers to lower transaction costs through shared transactions using pooled investing capital.

Both ETFs and Mutual funds have many individual securities and are regulated by the Securities Act of 1933, Securities Exchange Act of 1934, and the Investment Company Act of 1990. These laws were designed with the target of lowering the risk of a possible market crash like that of 1929.[35]

One key difference between the two funds is that mutual funds are traditionally designed to provide a wide range of choices while ETFs help to track an index. Here is a closer look at the two.

Mutual Funds

This is a type of managed investment that was first used in the US in 1924. Since then, they have become some of the

----

[35] Birdthistle, W, and Morney, J, 2018, *Research Handbook on the Regulation of Mutual Funds*. New York: Edward Edgar Publishing.

most preferred investment options for offering investors an extensive selection of pooled funds investment[36]. Note that though some are managed passively, the most preferred are those actively managed by top professionals.

As an investor, active management is an important parameter for helping to optimize the portfolio and returns.

It is important to note that actively managed mutual funds attract a high fee because the managers have to identify the best securities on behalf of the investor. The operational fee is expressed as a ratio that includes operational expenses, management fees, and 12B-1 fees. The 12B-1 fee is used to support expenses related to selling the fund via full-service brokerage. Notably, this fee is not charged in ETFs.

ETFs

ETFs started trading in 1993 and are, by law, required to be managed passively using securities tracking as an index. However, the US started allowing actively managed ETFs from 2008.

Traditionally, ETFs were very popular for index operators

---

[36] Anthan, N, 2016, Exchange-traded Funds and the New Dynamics of Investing. Oxford: Oxford University Press.

(traders) who targeted getting exposure to a specific segment of a market. Such traders mainly intended to diversify their portfolios. ETFs have evolved over time and yielded additional options such as the smart beta index funds.

When investing in ETFs, it is important to consider the associated fees. Though investors do not pay a sales load fee, they are required to remit a commission for trading them. Because ETFs are managed passively, the management fee is relatively low. As indicated earlier, ETFs do not charge 12b-1 fees. One outstanding ETF in the market is SPY.

SPY

Spy was created in January 1993 by State Street Global Advisors and became the first ETF to get listed in the US. It grew rapidly and became one of the top trading vehicles based on traded volume in the United States. The traded volume of the vehicle is about 80 million[37].

Traders hold SPY in high regard since it represents a group of 500 top US companies (S&P 500 Index) with total capitalization of more than five billion.

Each stock in the S&P 500 Index is required to be actively

---

[37] Anthan, N, 2016, Exchange-traded Funds and the New Dynamics of Investing. Oxford: Oxford University Press.

traded on its own. For investors, the tag (S&P 500 Index) is preferred because it offers better exposure to more companies with a single purchase.

Why Consider Investing in SPY?

The S&P 500 ETF is seen as an easy method for investors and traders to get access to the index that was initially only accessible to those who traded S&P 500 futures before the idea of SPY was created. However, it is important to appreciate that SPY offers more than simply access to an index. Indeed, a lot of ETFs offer access to index but operate way below SPY.

The longevity associated with SPY has made it to easily win the trust of fund managers (State Street). Indeed, traders are willing to trade on a daily basis because they are assured of high volumes that make it easy to open and close trades.

How does SPY Operate?

The S&P 500 works as a unit of trust. State Street buys and sells stocks to help align its pool holding in line with the S&P 500 index. This implies that when you purchase a SPY share, you are simply acquiring a unit that represents the stock of every S&P 500 index.

When investors purchase SPY, their anticipation is that the entire S&P 500 index value will go up. This means that investors can also sell their SPY units on the market at a profit. Note that if the holdings in the fund fall, the value of every SPY will also decline.

It is important to point that for day traders, the focus is not so much whether the index value will shift up or down. Because the S&P 500 stocks move the whole day, tracking SPY is a worthy undertaking. When the small movements are combined with large volumes, day traders capitalize on them to make profits.

Because SPY is traded on the stock market, a trader can decide to buy or sell some shares to or from other interested traders. Note that in some cases, the price of SPY might be too small to cause a major shift in the overall value of the S&P 500 index. However, fear or euphoria can make participants to push the price to record high or low.

If you want to know the actual value of SPY, make sure to check the symbol "SPY.NV every morning.

A Practical Sample Budget When Saving for Retirement

Learning to budget correctly is an important step to help you achieve financial freedom. The primary goal should be ensuring that you understand all the expenses and allocate them ample resources. Here is a sample budget:

Let assume that you are 30 years old and earning an annual income of $150,000 (12,500 monthly). This sample also assumes that you have made zero savings so far and target to retire at 65 years. Besides, you also target to live on 85% of the pre-retirement after retiring (this translates to $42,000).

To hit your goal, a total of $2 million will be needed by the time you retire. Though this could appear like it is a lot of money, it is not because it is spread over 35 years. Here is a breakdown of the budget.

Personal Budget for $12,500 for the month of March 2019	
Category (item)	Allocated Cost Per Item
1. Food	$3,000
2. Retirement scheme (401K)	$600
3. Roth IRA	$50
4. Emergency fund	$500
5. Student Loan	
6. Transport	$600
7. Holiday	$1,000
8. Family shopping	
9. New furniture	$6,00
10. New television	

11. Gifts	$2,000
12. Personal savings	$800
13. Miscellaneous	$400
	$300
	$1,500
	$650
	Total=$12,500

Housing versus Stock Market – the Truth

When people think of investment, two common options that click into their minds are Stocks and Housing. However, which is better between the two? Here is a comparison that seeks to demystify the benefits of each to help you pick the better option.

Real Estate

When you decide to invest in Real Estate, it implies that you are purchasing land or property. Note that some real estate options such as blank parcels of land could cost you more in property taxes even if no income is being generated.

Some properties that can generate cash for you include apartments, strip malls, and rental units. You could also

Steve E. Carruso

purchase property for improvement and sell later at a profit.

Pros and Investing in Real Estate

- Real estate is a comfortable option to invest in because you have always lived in a house. Therefore, you are conversant with some aspects of housing.
- When you channel resources to real estate, you will get something tangible. This sense of attachment allows you to stand a short distance away and say "that is my house".
- It is not easy to get defrauded when investing in properties because the process of ownership exchange is clearly defined. For example, transactions are completed by real estate attorneys or expert realtors.
- Properties provide you with full control over the investment. Whether you want to improve the houses, introduce new features, or even adjust the prices, you are the boss.

Cons of Real Estate

- Even if the property is not occupied, real estate will still attract some cost such as maintenance and property taxes.
- The return on real estate is very low. After inflation, you can be left with as little as 0% because of the high costs associated with maintaining the venture. For

example, you need to meet property taxes, insurance, utilities, maintenance, and toilet drains among others[38].

- You have to struggle with the management to sustain the real estate in top condition. If you prefer to hire a real estate manager, you will have to pay a fee (about 10% of the collected revenue).
- The process of acquiring or disposing of real estate investment is complex and lengthy. For example, you have to search for the preferred property, make physical visits, do a pre-purchase inspection, and wait for a couple of days before property lawyers can complete the transfer.

Stock Markets

Investing in stocks involves buying shares of selected companies and waiting to get a portion of the profit that they generate. It implies that whether the company of choice sells furniture, manufactures cars, deals with video games or offers tax services, you become part of it. For example, if a company has one million shares and you purchase 10,000,

---

[38] Rami, S, 2018, *Real Estate Investing: The Myths, facts, and ways to get started.* <available at> https://www.iwillteachyoutoberich.com/blog/surprising-real-estate-investing-myths/

you own 1% of the firm.

Pros of Investing in Stock Markets

- Investing in stock markets has been demonstrated for more than 100 years to be a great method of creating wealth. Even though the stock markets have undergone major depressive periods such as the infamous Stock Market Crash of 1929, they easily spring back to offer profits to investors.
- When you buy stocks of a company, you are entitled to getting a share of the generated profit without getting directly involved. This implies that you can purchase the shares and only come back at the end of the year to check the profit they have generated. You will not be required to get directly involved with the management.
- Apart from the cost of buying the shares, there are no additional expenses. Unlike the real estates that will require some maintenance costs even when no income is generated, stock markets are stress-free.
- Investing in stock markets is very easy. Indeed, you can follow the performance of a company and buy its shares online at the comfort of your home. Besides, you can also sell the shares within minutes.
- If you select high-quality stocks, they will generate both profit and dividends at the end of the year. Take

the case of Johnson & Johnson that started trading in 1944. If you bought one share when in 1944 when the cost was $37.50 and held it to date, the value would have gone up an impressive 17%.

- With stocks, it is very easy to diversity. For example, you can invest directly in companies that are performing well in the market or other high return ventures such as mutual funds. Mutual funds allow you to invest as little as $100 per month and rake in huge profits.

- Like real estate, you can borrow cash against your stocks. The only thing that is needed is approval from your trading broker.

Cons of Capital Markets

- Though stocks promise high returns, they can experience extreme fluctuations, especially in the short term. Therefore, it is advisable to only invest in top companies and diversifying your funds onto different types of stocks such as mutual funds, ETFs and stocks.

- When you purchase stocks, you do not have something tangible to associate with. This means that though you own part of a major company, it is not possible to stand there and say this is my company.

- Though you are part of a selected company after

buying its shares, you do not have control over it. Instead, the company operates under different management that manages the daily operations.

Though both real estate and stock markets have unique benefits, stocks provide a better option to rake in more revenue. They are also easy to acquire, diversify, and even dispose.

Chapter Eight: Making Credit Cards Work for you

Credit cards are some of the most used methods of payment in the United States today. They are preferred by many people because they are widely accepted in many stores and you can pay without having to carry cash in a wallet.

A lot of people also like the cards because they can spend more than they have. This makes credit card a reliable tool for shopping during emergencies or when you have financial shortfalls. Even with these advantages, credit cards have become like a trap that funnels people to debts. It is estimated that more than 22% of Americans have more credit card debts than savings[39].

This chapter takes a closer look at credit cards to establish how to make them work for you. It explores how the credit card companies make money, and how you can build your credit score. Finally, it outlines the common credit cards in the market that you should consider using today.

---

[39] Megan, E, 2017, *15 Scary Facts about Debt that Should Alarm you.* <available at> https://www.cheatsheet.com/money-career/facts-about-debt-may-alarm-you-today.html/

Steve E. Carruso

How Credit Card Companies Make Money

The large number of Americans with credit card loans leads to one key question: "How do credit card companies generate revenue?" Before looking at the method used by credit card companies to make money, it is important to understand how they work.

Credit card companies comprise of two types of enterprises; networks and issuers.

- Issuers: These are credit unions and banks that issue the credit cards. This means that when you use a credit card, you are simply borrowing cash from an issuer. Even retail credit cards that come with the name of a specific brand such as gas station or merchant are still issued by banks that have entered into a contract with the respective retailer[40].
- Networks: These are companies that process transactions done via credit cards. Major networks in the United States today include Visa and American Express. However, Discover and American Express are both issuers and networks.

---

[40] Abel, G, 2018, Amazing Credit Repair: Boost Your Credit Score, Use Loopholes (Section 609), and Overcome Credit Card Debt Forever. New York: CreateSpace Independent Publishing Platform

When you make payments using a credit card, it is relayed via multiple parties. The transaction is initiated by the issuer, via the network and finally to the merchant bank. Therefore, the network has to ensure that every transaction is linked to the right card holder.

Credit card companies make money in three key ways: interest, fees, and interchange.

Interest

Most of the credit card companies make their cash from interest payments. It is possible to avoid interest on your credit card by ensuring that the balance is paid on time and in full. However, the interest can accrue when it is carried from one month to another.

Interchange

When you used a credit card for payment, the accepting store has to pay a processing fee that is equivalent to the percentage of the involved transaction. A portion of this fee is credited to the credit card issuer using the payment network. It ranges between 1% and 3% and is referred to as an interchange fee. The fee is set by the network and varies depending on the involved volume and value of the transaction.

Steve E. Carruso

Fees

Subprime credit card issuers that specialize with clients who have bad credit make the bulk of their money from fees compared to interests. However, mass-market credit card issuers have a wide range of fees including the following:

- **Annual fee:** This fee is charged on cards that have high reward rates and people with poor credit scores.
- **Cash advance fees:** This fee is charged by issuers when clients use their cards to withdraw funds from ATM. The fee is approximately 3.5% of the cash being withdrawn.
- **Balance transfer fee:** This fee is charged when you transfer debt from one card to another. The interest ranges from 3% to 5% of the amount that you transfer.
- **Late fees:** If you do not pay the minimum amount by the right date, a later charge fee will be attached to your card.

Building Your Credit Score without Falling into Debt

A credit score is a three digit number that is used to describe how likely a person is to repay a debt. The score is used by lenders and banks when making decisions about the loans to approve or decline[41].

The score is calculated by three credit reporting agencies, Equifax, TransUnion, and Experian based on your financial operations. The agencies work with lenders and companies that you do business with to gather information to use when calculating your credit score. Here are the different types of information that the credit reporting agencies use to calculate your score:

- Your payment history
- The length of time you have had credit
- The amount of debt that you have
- How you are using credit limits
- Type of credit that you have (example, mortgage, student loan, and credit cards among others)

How to Build Your Credit Score without Getting into Debt

When you improve your credit score, you will not be looked at as a high-risk party by financial institutions and other companies that use the score to offer specific services. You

---

[41] Credit Karma, 2019, *How to Understand Credit score.* <available at> https://www.creditkarma.com/credit-scores/

will even enjoy lower interest rates on the loans provided to you. Here are the top methods that you should use to strengthen credit score without getting into debt.

- **Pay credit card balance in full.** Because credit score assesses your ability to manage debt, it is important to maintain good record of timely payments. Make sure you understand your credit card balance and pay it in full without letting it overflow to the next month. Note that this will also save you interest charges.

- **Consider credit cards like debit cards.** One risk associated with credit cards is that your bank account balance does not change when you process payment in a store. It only changes when you pay the credit card bill. Therefore, it is easy to lose track of the amount you are spending.

To avoid this scenario, you need to maintain a budget indicating when to use the card and when not to. If you know how much the card allows you to spend, treat it like a debit card.

- **Leverage credit card options.** Leveraging the credit card is used to help strengthen the credit score and avoid the pitfalls that can pull it down. First, you should carefully manage your debt-to-credit ratio. It is advisable to keep the debt below 30% of the available credit line.

You can also go for credit transfer. This is a good option when you are trying to pay your credit card balance. Transferring balance will help you to clear balance easily and improve the debt-to-credit ratio.

- **Keep Your Credit Card for a Long Time.**
  Keeping your credit card over a long period especially if it has good standing will help to pull the score up.

Factors that can Damage Your Credit Score

A credit score is perhaps the most important thing about your finances because it determines your ability to access credit from financial institutions. Even if you have a good business idea and want to bridge the financial gap through a bank loan, the request might be turned away if the credit score is poor. Here are the different things that can damage (pull down) your credit score:

- **Missing your loan repayment:** If you are late to repay your loan by more than 30 days, you will be reported to the credit reference bureaus such as Equifax. Then, your credit score will be recalculated and pulled down factoring the late repayment.
- **Requesting too many credit card reports:** Though requesting a credit card report is important to

identify errors and getting them corrected, multiple requests gives the impression that you are desperate for credit. This will pull down the credit score.

- **Bankruptcy:** If you are declared bankrupt, your credit score will fall with a huge margin. It can drop by up to 240 points. Besides, bankruptcy can stay on the report for more than 10 years[42].

- **Tax lien:** If you have an unpaid tax debt, it will damage your credit score by a huge margin of up to 240 points.

- **Debt consolidation:** When you apply for debt consolidation, it implies that you are unable to service all your lines of credit. It will pull down the credit score with a significant margin.

- **Credit report errors:** If your credit report contains errors such as wrong entries or missing information about your financial details, the credit score is likely to be incorrect.

Important Steps for Rebuilding/building Your Credit Score

If your credit score gets damaged by things such as late loan

---

[42] Baverley, Harzog, 2015, The Debt Escape Plan: How to Free Yourself From Credit Card Balances, Boost Your Credit Score, and Live Debt-Free. Washington: Red Wheel Weiser.

repayment or even bankruptcy, it is very important to consistently rebuild it. Here are useful tips you can use:

- **Start by checking your credit report and correcting errors.** One thing you need to appreciate is that credit reporting agencies that calculate your score rely on the info provided to them by other parties like banks. Therefore, if they have the wrong information or some reports are missing, the credit score will be incorrect[43]. So, you should always start by checking the credit report for errors and having them corrected immediately.

Note that you do not have to pay to get a credit report. Every 12 months, you are entitled to get a free copy of your credit report from AnnualCreditReport.com.

- **Use a Secured credit card:** If you use a standard credit card, controlling spending can be an uphill task. This could easily get you into debts and pull down the credit score. Instead, you should consider going for a secured credit card. This is a type of credit card that requires you to make an upfront deposit to prevent overspending. This is a great way to stay within your

---

43 Baverley, Harzog, 2015, The Debt Escape Plan: How to Free Yourself From Credit Card Balances, Boost Your Credit Score, and Live Debt-Free. Washington: Red Wheel Weiser.

budget and rebuild credit score.

- **Pay your bills on time:** There is a general perception that it is only bank credit and mortgage that can be reported to the credit reporting agencies. But this is wrong. If you fail to pay your power, water and gas bills on time, they can also pull down the score. Therefore, you should always ensure that such bills are paid on time.

- **Keep old financial accounts active:** It is advisable to be smart with credit cards by avoiding closing the card accounts. When your report has a higher average age on the credit card accounts, the credit score will go up. It is also advisable to avoid opening many credit cards within a short time because it can be interpreted that you are eager for credit.

- **Try to maintain the same level of activity with your card:** If your credit card is inactive or gets closed, it will push down the credit score. Instead, you should keep the credit cards active even if you only use it to make minimum purchases to keep it on.

- **Ensure to prudently manage your finances:** Even as you use the credit card to rebuild your credit score, it is important to appreciate that even activities in other areas such as student loan or medical credit can still push it down[44]. Therefore, manage your finances prudently to avoid falling into debts that can suddenly pull down the score. It is especially crucial to ensure you have emergency funds to cater for unexpected occurrences such as medical emergencies. Make sure that your family also has medical insurance coverage.

Now that you know how to build your credit score using a credit card without falling into debt, it is also important to have the right cards. Here are the main types of credit cards you should consider.

1) **Citi Double Card:** This card offers 2% cash back on every single purchase that you make. It is considered the best cash back card on the market because it does not have revolving categories or annual fees.

2) **Amex Blue Cash Preferred**: This card charges annual fee of $75 per year, but offers 6% cash back on the groceries (with a cap), 3% on gas stations, and 1% on everything else. This card can be a great option for families that spend a lot on groceries and gas.

---

[44] Ibid

Chapter Nine: Side Hustles & Making Money Online

One question that might be lingering at the back of the mind is; "How can I reach financial freedom fast?" One of the answers to the question is creating multiple sources of passive income. The additional revenue can be used to knock down your debts fast, build savings, and even expand your business.

This chapter demonstrates how to make streams of income and explores different methods you can use to make money online. As you look for investment opportunities, the chapter also demonstrates how to spot and avoid pyramid schemes.

What is Passive Income and Multiple Streams of Revenue?

The concepts of passive income and multiple streams of revenue are important when working towards financial freedom. Passive income is income that you generate on a regular basis but with minimum effort to maintain it.

Having multiple streams of revenue especially, of passive income, is very important when building wealth. Whether you are at your workplace or home, the different streams of revenue keep funneling money to your portfolio.

The main reason for creating passive income is because it is not connected to your time. This implies that you can still be engaged in doing other tasks such as creating new streams of income.

One thing that you need to appreciate about passive income is that it does not need to be a lot of money. The little you can make will go a long way to helping grow your finances. Think of a passive line of income that generates $500 a month. Though it might look small, it could go a long way to help build long term savings.

In a year, your $500 will have reached $6,000 which could be enough to clear part of your student loan, mortgage or other debt. Indeed, if your debt requires you to only pay $500 or less per month, the passive income could cater for it so that your main income can go into other areas such building new businesses or an emergency fund.

Three Steps to Creating Multiple Streams of Passive Revenue

To create multiple streams of revenue, here are three proven steps that you should consider.

1. Start by Picking One Stream of Revenue You are Passionate about

The first stream of revenue should be something that you

love. This is because the first stream of revenue could be the toughest since you had not been engaged in a similar venture before[45].

Note that you might need to take time learning about the stream of revenue. Depending on the selected channel, it might be important to start by setting the parameters of operations such as the services on sale, the audience, and the targeted niche.

By selecting a stream that you are passionate about, it implies that you can wait until the income starts flowing. If the first stream of income works for you, it might be possible to diversify to others.

2. Systemize the First Stream of Income

After perfecting the first stream of revenue, go ahead and systematize it so that only your limited attention and time will be needed. This is done by using appropriate human resources and technologies. You are simply leaving other people or automating the system so that you can concentrate on creating new streams of income.

Before you can fully hand over, make sure to pre-test the new

---

[45] The Financial Mentor, 2019, *Multiple Streams of Revenue: The Truth Revealed.* <available at>https://financialmentor.com/wealth-building/wealth-program-system/multiple-streams-of-income/13096

team or automation to get the assurance that operations will run effectively and create the targeted revenue.

3. Leverage Resources to Create Additional Streams of Income

Once the first stream of income starts generating revenue without taking much of your time, then you will now have ample time and energy to build the next stream of income. The skills and knowledge that you gained in the first stream of revenue are crucial when building the next source of income.

Because you took time learning how the first stream of income works, you will not need to start from scratch when working on new streams. If you create an online application and design a website to sell it, it will be easier to market newer apps because you could still use the same site. Creating newer streams of revenue will be easier and faster compared to the first one.

Opportunities you can exploit to make Passive Income

Today, there are many opportunities that you can exploit to add new streams of revenue to your financial portfolio. Here are some of them:

Steve E. Carruso

1. *Affiliate Marketing*

Affiliate marketing is a performance-based type of marketing where a business uses affiliates to market its product. Then, the affiliate marketer is paid a commission when a client he brings buys the product under consideration[46]. It is a cheap way for you to start making money online without creating your own product.

How Does Affiliate Marketing Work?

To be successful as an affiliate marketer, you need to identify a niche of interest and build a large following. You can do this by establishing yourself as an authority to win a large and loyal following. This can also be achieved through writing content about the niche of interest and engaging the community to win its trust.

Once you have created a loyal following, you will need to select a good Affiliate Marketing program such as WordPress Affiliate Manager or Shortlinks. These programs help to track your performance and carefully follow clients who purchase after your persuasion.

It is also important to set your affiliate marketing channels

---

[46] Marketing Artfully, 2019, How to add affiliate marketing as a revenue stream <available at>https://marketingartfully.com/add-affiliate-marketing-revenue-stream/

where you can recommend products to your followers. This means your website and marketing email list. You can also install third-party plugins such as Post Affiliate Pro and ShareSale to help you to evaluate the level of success.

Useful Tips to Help You Become A Pro Affiliate Manager

One fact you need to appreciate when starting an affiliate marketing program is that it is not a get-rich-overnight venture. Today, affiliate marketing has become highly competitive. Therefore, you need to carefully build your portfolio to win the trust of both followers and businesses. Here are some useful tips to help you succeed in affiliate marketing.

- **It is advisable to only work with a few products:** The first mistake that you can make in affiliate marketing is picking too many products or trying to promote everything. The problem with this approach is that you are likely to get overwhelmed. Instead, you should only pick a few items that you can easily promote and convince your followers to purchase.
- **Use multiple traffic sources for product promotion:** In many cases, affiliate marketers only put the ads on their sites and blogs. But this is the wrong way to do it because people who are not visiting your site are likely to miss the ads.

The ideal marketing method is reaching the target audience via multiple channels. You should particularly maintain a presence on the top social media pages such as Facebook and Instagram. Other channels include your blog, YouTube, and Guest pages.

- **Make sure to comprehensively research the demand of the target product:** Though you want to make money via affiliate marketing, you cannot simply pick any item because the manufacturer has placed a request. To know the right product to promote, you need to research its demand.

Take a bit of your time analyzing the product's demand. The goal is picking an item that is easy to market instead of a product that is likely to get rejected. Ensure to follow the product development process and also tie it with the image of the manufacturer.

- **Aim at strengthening your followers' base:** Even though the primary target of affiliate marketing is creating additional income, it is important to look at the venture from a long term perspective. Though you are recommending products of other companies, try to maintain buyers as part of your community.

To build a lasting community, the focus should be providing the correct status of the items you recommend as opposed to simply market it. If you find that a product is lacking in one way or another, decline marketing it. This honesty will ensure that you always have huge following and products to market.

Pros of Affiliate Marketing

- No investment is needed to create your own products
- There is a wide range of products to be promoted
- Customer service is the role of the businesses seeking your affiliate marketing services
- It is a high-income potential channel
- Allows you to sell complementary products simultaneously. For example, you can sell your own products and those of the contracting businesses

Cons of Affiliate Marketing

- You lack control over a lot of things in the marketing process. These include product features, updates, and price.
- Building a trustworthy following is not easy. It could take months or even years.

2. *Blogging*

Blogs were originally created as platforms for helping brands build communities and making regular communications with the target audience. However, they have evolved to become top marketing platforms for businesses and individuals. Here is an account of how you can create a new stream of revenue through blogging.

Identify a Blogging Niche

Even before you can set up a blog, it is important to pick up one or several niches that you want to blog about. This will help to present yourself as an expert and mold you into an authority over time[47].

To pick the right niche, it is advisable to pick the area you are passionate about. For example, if you have an interest in fitness, consider blogging on niches such as weight management and fitness training. Other areas of consideration can be human resources management, pregnancy, early childhood development, and education.

After selecting the preferred niche, start researching it to understand the target audience, its preferences, and other players. This will help you to craft a winning approach to draw high traffic and create interest from companies.

Create Your Blogging Platform

Now that you have decided about the area of interest, you

---

[47] ProBlogger, 2017, *Make Money Blogging*. <available at> https://problogger.com/make-money-blogging/

need to create a blog. This is a platform just like a website but that is mainly used for communication and liaison with the target audience. Though you could engage a web developer to create a winning blog, it is also possible to create one from scratch.

Top Content Management System (CMS) platforms such as WordPress allow you to create a new blog from scratch in just a few clicks. They have multiple templates that come with most features such as content publishing and search engine optimization (SEO) that will come in handy once your blog starts running.

You will also need to host your blog using companies such as GoDaddy and HostGator. Ensure to pick the hosting provider that guarantees fast loading and high uptime of more than 99.99%. Note that the hosting provider will also charge a small fee for hosting the blog. The average hosting cost today is about $2.5/ month.

Start Creating and Publishing Content on Your Blog

Now that your blog is live, you need to start creating content to draw traffic and build a community. Most of the people visiting your blog will be looking for engaging content that educates, entertains, and guides them. Therefore, it is important to interact with the target audience and understand what it wants.

Your content should be comprehensively researched to progressively build you as an authority in the niche. Make sure to target different areas of the selected niche and post content regularly to keep the audience coming back for more.

Note that once the blog starts running, it will not be enough to drive traffic on its own. You need to share it and the content with other websites, blogs, and social media platforms. This will help to draw a lot of traffic to the blog. When the blog following grows to thousands, companies will start developing an interest in reaching them.

Start Making Money Online

Just like in affiliate marketing, it is important to appreciate that blogging requires ample time to start generating income. Therefore, the main goal should be building an engaged audience that views you as an authority. Then, use the following strategies to generate revenue:

- **Make income from advertising:** This is the starting point for most bloggers' website monetization. Because of the large following coming to your blog, you will be viewed as a perfect point for companies to place advertisements. Now, you can charge them based on the nature and time of the ad.
- **Start generating affiliate income:** Now that you have a loyal following, you could create another

stream of revenue via affiliate marketing. Here, you will be marketing products from other companies to your audience and getting paid some commission when your referrals make purchases.

- **Run events and charge a fee:** Though advertising is the main line of revenue for most bloggers, holding events can help raise even more income. Running online events such as conferences at specific intervals and charging attendants a fee can generate a lot of revenue.

The good thing with blogging events is that they can be attended by viewers from across the world. This implies that you are not restricted by administrative boundaries and, therefore, can generate a lot of income.

- **Develop recurring income with the blog:** Because most of your followers come to read content, you can create a channel of recurring income by creating membership programs. The members are allowed to access top-notch content, tools, or a combination of services for a monthly or annual cost. Note that this stream of income revenue would require you to also generate high-quality content for the members.
- **Create own products to sell on the blog:** If you are an expert in a specific area, you can generate a

product such as a guide, app or ebook and sell to the followers. For example, a fitness enthusiast can sell an ebook guide for cutting weight and staying healthy. Though such ebooks take time to create, they can generate a lot of income over time.

Pros of Blogging

- Provides high potential for making a lot of money
- You can create multiple streams of revenue using blogging
- It requires a limited amount of money to set up and start generating money
- You can also sell own digital products and services such as ebooks, guides, tools, and applications

Cons of Blogging

- Logging requires a lot of time to create and start earning a lot of money. First, you have to build yourself as an authority and drive a huge following
- Today, blogging has become very competitive. This makes it even harder to outdo competitors and start earning the cash you want

3. *Self-Publishing Books*

In the past, thoughts of making a publication were complex and, seemingly, out of reach for many people. However, the emergence of self-publishing platforms like Amazon has now made it easy for you to write a book of choice and publish it for millions of viewers across the globe to read. Think of this as a unique opportunity to reach millions of readers and sell them your book.

To start making money on Amazon, you need to sign up for a free Kindle Direct Publishing (KDP) account that allows you to create and add new books within minutes. The account simply requires you to fill the title of the book, author name, cover, description, the book price, and the book before clicking publish. Then, your book will be reviewed in about 24 hours before getting published.

When Amazon sells your book, it pays you a royalty of 70%. Here is a complete guide on how to make money through self-publishing books on Amazon:

Identify a Profitable Category

To make money publishing books at Amazon, you only need to look for areas that attract a lot of interest. Think of your area of interest such as fitness, employment, value addition, money management, and relationships. You could even start by exploring the challenges facing the targeted audience and create a book to address them.

It is important to appreciate that as a self-publishing portal, the competition is very high. Therefore, getting a high-value

Steve E. Carruso

niche with low competition can be your gateway to generating a lot of income.

Evaluate the Profitability of the Book Ideas

One mistake that you should avoid making is assuming that there is a ready market for whatever book you publish on Amazon. Before you can start creating the book of interest, it is important to carry comprehensive research on Amazon and other platforms such as Google Books. For example, you can simply search the title of the book you want to write on the Amazon Kindle to see similar works with the same ideas.

Create Your Book Title and Cover

After choosing a niche of interest, the next step should be coming up with a title and book cover. Make sure to have a catchy keyword included in the title so that clients searching for related info can easily pick it. If your primary keyword is something like "acne treatment", a good title could be *"Acne Treatment-The Simple, Tested, and Proven Ways to Cure Acne Fast."*

Write your Book and Publish

Now that you have the right niche, the right title, and an Amazon Kindle account, it is time to get down and write the book. Make sure to carefully present the ideas so that readers will find the book enjoyable to read. This way, they will even recommend it to colleagues and friends.

You can also hire other people to write the book on your behalf. This is a great way to handle high-value topics that are out of your area of specialization. Consider checking for freelance writers on top writing platforms such as Upwork and WarriorForum.

Once the book is ready, it is time to publish it so that readers can see, buy, and read. To get more people to read the book, you should consider giving it away to a number of people and ask them to leave reviews.

Pros of Self-Publishing Books on Amazon

- Fast exposure of your content
- High potential for a lot of revenue
- Longer shelf life of your books
- The process of publishing is easy once you complete a book

Cons of Self-Publishing Books on Amazon

- There is less editorial and marketing support.

4. *Private Labeling with Amazon FBA*

Private labeling is one of the new methods that could generate a lot of money for you. It is a business model where you sell products on Amazon under your own label. Once you have studied a product of interest and market, you simply go ahead and contact the manufacturer to produce it and sell on Amazon under your brand name[48]. This is awesome.

Many people like the idea of being able to market different products under their labels because they can operate like big stores and make a lot of profit without leaving their house. To make more through private labeling, it is advisable to select a product that has a lot of demand.

Pros of Private Labeling

- You are allowed to sell any product on the giant Amazon e-commerce website
- You do not have to worry about product production
- Private labeling has huge potential for high income

Cons of Private Labeling

- You do not have direct control over the product content such as taste and dimensions

Economies of Scale of digital vs physical products

---

[48] Randy, B, 2017, *Your Amazon Label Guide for Passive Income, Part 1.* <available at> https://medium.com/@randybechtold/your-amazon-fba-private-label-guide-for-passive-income-part-1-eb5b53a031c6

When deciding on the multiple streams of revenue to consider, you might be wondering whether to sell digital or physical products. The main focus should be the ability to generate as many products as possible and pushing them to the target audience without cost limitations[49].

- **Digital Products:** These are products that exist in an intangible format. The products are highly scalable because once you create one, it can be reproduced into millions of copies at no extra cost. For example, if you create a book to sell online, millions of clients can download it without affecting the original copy.
- **Physical products:** If you opt to sell physical products, the economies of scale will be poor because of the high cost of production. For example, the process of creating a detergent requires physical facilities, human labor, and actual transportation from the manufacturer to the seller[50]. The complex production and supply chains of physical products make it difficult to generate significant revenue.

Because multiple streams of revenue should be able to work effectively without taking a lot of your time, it is advisable to

[49] Mark, G, 2019, *Digital Economies at Global Margins*. Cambridge, Ma: MIt Press.

[50] Ibid

consider dealing with digital products. If you create a book, it can keep generating income for many years without incurring additional costs.

Multi-Level Marketing Traps: How to Spot and Avoid Them

Multi-Level Marketing companies, or in practical terms, pyramid schemes, are "get rich quick" schemes that are run by a small group of people that want to steal from unsuspecting investors. In a common pyramid scheme, this group of scammers is at the "apex of the pyramid"[51].

The first pyramid scheme was run by Charles Ponzi who created a "top-down" scam that promised promissory notes of 50% interest in three months to investors. During the scam, Ponzi made $15 million.[52]

- How Do Pyramids Schemes Work

Pyramids commence with an originator who sits at the top of the scheme. He puts a small amount of money into the scheme and advertises it as a great opportunity to make

---

[51] Robert, F, 2019, Ponziomics: The Untold story of Multi-Level Marketing and How Direct Selling Became an American Swindle. New York: FitzPatrick Management Incorporated.

[52] Ibid

quick money. The idea is to look like the organization is selling a product or service but the primary goal is to convince people to join and charge them a fee.

Because you are promised repayment at a high-interest rate, the new people joining the pyramid provide the cash needed to pay the early investors. The schemes even generate financial accounts, profit statements, and anything that can depict them as genuine operators.

The last moment of a pyramid scheme is when it grows and becomes impossible to pay investors. When the early investors cash out, it becomes impossible to pay those at the bottom of the pyramid[53]. When investors realize there is no cash to pay them, the pyramid simply collapses.

- How to Identify and Avoid MLM Pyramid Schemes

To avoid losing your money through pyramid schemes, you should be able to easily identify them and stay away. Here are some of the indicators to look for:

1. **Look for high-pressure investment environment:** The pyramid initiators and marketers want to make it seem as if you are going to miss a very

---

[53] Robert, F, 2019, Ponziomics: The Untold story of Multi-Level Marketing and How Direct Selling Became an American Swindle. New York: FitzPatrick Management Incorporated.

big opportunity that will never come back in life. The aim of this is making you hand over money without carefully investigating the investment opportunity under consideration.

2. **Being required to sign up via other people:** If you find an investment venture that is requiring you to sign-up via another person, the chances are that it is a pyramid. The person seeking to recruit you has been promised good returns if he introduces new members so that they can pay and keep growing the pyramid.

3. **Pyramid schemes involve selling cheap services or products:** If you take a closer look at the products being sold by the organization and note they are of poor quality and are not sold via the conventional marketing channels like retail lines, the chances are that it is a pyramid scheme[54]. Here, you should ask questions such as; "If the product is so good, has it been approved by relevant authorities?" and "Why is it not common in the market?"

4. **An upfront fee or large capital is required:** If you are required to make a specific initial deposit

---

[54] Robert, F, 2019, Ponziomics: The Untold story of Multi-Level Marketing and How Direct Selling Became an American Swindle. New York: FitzPatrick Management Incorporated.

promising very high returns, it is time to take a moment and think about it. For example, if an investment opportunity promises 50% returns in just a few months; try to ask the nature of the investment with such super returns. When the deal is too good to be true, make sure to think twice.

Popular MLM Companies

- Advocare
- Arbonne
- Monat
- Avon
- Cutco
- DoTERRA
- LuLaRoe
- Lipsense
- Amway
- Young Living
- Mary Kay
- Scentsy
- Rodan + Fields

Conclusion

You do not have to have a lot of money to live a large life. However, being liberated from debts will usher you into a new phase of financial freedom and success. The problem of debt is reeling because people do not take the right approaches to address it. However, you are a powerhouse and can overcome it.

From an early stage in life, people are ushered into the life of debt such that they rarely acknowledge it getting out of control. However, this book has demonstrated that it is possible to emerge from debt and blast through into the millionaire you always wanted to be.

Once you create the right mindset to clear the debt, everything else will start falling into place. You also need to cut unnecessary spending and direct cash to addressing the debt. If you are using the right model such as the 4-step debt eliminator, the process of knocking the debt off will become easier as loans get cleared one at a time.

As you move out of debt, it is important to start creating multiple streams of revenue and investing in different areas. Do not wallow in debts, there is a way out.If you follow the advice in this book over a consistent period of time, you will be in a much better position than 95% of people.

Bibliography

Abel, G, 2018, Amazing Credit Repair: Boost Your Credit Score, Use Loopholes (Section 609), and Overcome Credit Card Debt Forever. New York: CreateSpace Independent Publishing Platform

Adam, H, *21+ Motivational Stories About Getting out of Debt*. <available at> https://adamhagerman.com/21-get-out-of-debt-stories/

Anthan, N, 2016, Exchange-traded Funds and the New Dynamics of Investing. Oxford: Oxford University Press.

Baverley, Harzog, 2015, The Debt Escape Plan: How to Free Yourself From Credit Card Balances, Boost Your Credit Score, and Live Debt-Free. Washington: Red Wheel Weiser.

Birdthistle, W, and Morney, J, 2018, *Research Handbook on the Regulation of Mutual Funds*. New York: Edward Edgar Publishing.

Chatterjee, A, 2016, Is the statement of Murphy's Law valid? *Complexity*, 21 (6): 374–380.

Claire, B, 2019, *How 401K Matching Works*. <available at>https://www.investopedia.com/articles/personal-finance/112315/how-401k-matching-works.asp

Credit Karma, 2019, *How to Understand Credit score.*

Steve E. Carruso

<available at> https://www.creditkarma.com/credit-scores/

CreditLoan, 2019, How Debt Affects Relationships and What to Do About It. <available at> https://www.creditloan.com/blog/how-debt-affects-relationships/

Digangi, C, 2015, *The Scary Link Between Credit Card Debt and Depression.* <available at> http://money.com/money/3848551/credit-card-debt-depression/

Disease called Debt, 2018, *Debt Success Stories: Richard Paid off $40,000 in Debt.* <Available at>https://diseasecalleddebt.com/debt-success-stories-richard/

Jim, W, 2019, *Best Personal Finance Software apps of 2019.* <available at> https://wallethacks.com/best-personal-finance-software-apps/

Judith, O, 2018, *How this Couple Paid Off Nearly $162,000 Of Debt In 3 Years.* <Available at > https://www.refinery29.com/en-us/2018/03/194339/how-one-couple-paid-off-all-their-debt

Marketing Artfully, 2019, How to add affiliate marketing as a revenue stream <available at>https://marketingartfully.com/add-affiliate-marketing-revenue-stream/

Mark, G, 2019, *Digital Economies at Global Margins*. Cambridge, Ma: MIT Press.

Megan, E, 2017, *15 Scary Facts about Debt that Should Alarm you.* <available at> https://www.cheatsheet.com/money-career/facts-about-debt-may-alarm-you-today.html/

Nerdwallet, 201, *What is Roth IRA.* <available at> https://www.nerdwallet.com/article/what-is-a-roth-ira

Previte, J, and Hoffman, R, 2014, *Essential Financial Mathematics*. Washington: Lulu.com

ProBlogger, 2017, *Make Money Blogging.* <available at> https://problogger.com/make-money-blogging/

Randy, B, 2017, *Your Amazon Label Guide for Passive Income, Part 1.* <available at> https://medium.com/@randybechtold/your-amazon-fba-private-label-guide-for-passive-income-part-1-eb5b53a031c6

Ramsey, D, 2013, The Total Money Makeover: A Proven Plan for Financial Fitness. London: Thomas Nelson

Robert, F, 2019, Ponziomics: The Untold story of Multi-Level Marketing and How Direct Selling Became an American Swindle. New York: FitzPatrick Management Incorporated.

Steve E. Carruso

RothIRA.co.m, 2019, *Roth IRA Limits.* <available at> https://www.rothira.com/roth-ira-limits

The Balance, 2019, *How to Calculate Annual Percentage Rate (APR).* <available at >https://www.thebalance.com/annual-percentage-rate-apr-315533

The Financial Mentor, 2019, *Multiple Streams of Revenue: The Truth Revealed.* <available at>https://financialmentor.com/wealth-building/wealth-program-system/multiple-streams-of-income/13096

www.ingramcontent.com/pod-product-compliance
Lightning Source LLC
Chambersburg PA
CBHW071702210326
41597CB00017B/2286